TWAYNE'S WORLD AUTHORS SERIES (TWAS)

The purpose of TWAS is to survey the major writers —novelists, dramatists, historians, poets, philosophers, and critics—of the nations of the world. Among the national literatures covered are those of Australia, Canada, China, Eastern Europe, France, Germany, Greece, India, Italy, Japan, Latin America, the Netherlands, New Zealand, Poland, Russia, Scandinavia, Spain, and the African nations, as well as Hebrew, Yiddish, and Latin Classical literatures. This survey is complemeted by Twayne's United States Authors Series and English Authors Series

The intent of each volume in these series is to present a critical-analytical study of the works of the writer; to include biographical and historical material that may be necessary for understanding, appreciation, and critical appraisal of the writer; and to present all material in clear, concise English—but not to vitiate the scholarly content of the work by doing so.

ABOUT THE AUTHOR

I. L. McClelland is Reader in Spanish at the University of Glasgow, Britain, and a writer of several books on eighteenth-century Spanish literature. Her most recent publications are *Benito Jerónimo Feijoo* (Twayne, New York, 1969) and the two-volume *Spanish Drama of Pathos 1750-1808* (Liverpool University Press, 1970).

TWAYNE'S WORLD AUTHORS SERIES

A Survey of the World's Literature

Sylvia E. Bowman, Indiana University

GENERAL EDITOR

SPAIN

Gerald Wade, Vanderbilt University

EDITOR

Ignacio de Luzán

(TWAS 221)

Ignacio de Luzán

By IVY L. McCLELLAND

University of Glasgow

Twayne Publishers, Inc.   ::   New York

To
Professor William C. Atkinson
With Respect and Gratitude

Preface

Luzán is a well-known name in the history of Spanish literature, though his work is seldom read or discussed. We have tried to show that it is worth studying as an intelligent expression of its epoch. His *Poetics*, an important treatise on aesthetic philosophy, has been largely—and very ably—studied so far for the determination of its foreign sources. Our own chief aim has been, while allowing for foreign influences, to analyze the ideological significance of the *Poetics* in its Spanish context; to relate it to Luzán's minor works which are interesting in their own right; and to observe his capacity throughout his life for intellectual and creative development.

Contents

Contents

Chronology

1702   March 28: Born in Zaragoza, Aragon, Spain.

1715   Sent to join his uncle, Josef de Luzán, in Mallorca.

1715–   Traveled and studied in various parts of Italy, including
1727   Genoa, Milan, Naples, and Palermo.

1727   Graduated as Doctor of Laws in University of Catania.

1729   On death of Josef de Luzán, Don Ignacio took up residence with his brother Count Luzán in Naples.

1733   Returned to Zaragoza to administer Count Luzán's estates.

ca. 1737   Married Doña María Francisca Mincholet.

1737   Publication in Zaragoza of *La Poética* (*Poetics*).

1741–   Made Honorary and later Associate Member of the
1742   Royal Academy of the Spanish Language. Some short time afterwards became Member of the Spanish Royal Academy of History.

1742   Wrote the play *La virtud coronada* (*Virtue Crowned*) for performance in Monzón, Aragon.

1741–   Engaged in historical treatises, translation, and original
1747   poetry.

1747   Translated by commission *The Clemency of Titus* from *La Clemenza di Tito* of Metastasio for royal performance.

1747–   Held a senior post in the Spanish Embassy in Paris and
1750   was in charge of the Embassy from September, 1749 to May, 1750. Returned to Madrid.

1750–   Held various government posts including Superinten-
1754   dent of the Spanish Mint and Treasurer of the Royal Library.

1751 Admitted as Member of the Academy of Good Taste in Madrid. Publication of the *Memorias literarias de París* (*Paris Memoirs*) and of *La razón contra la moda* (*Reason Versus Convention*) translated from La Chaussée.

1752 Admitted as Member of the Academy of San Fernando and as Honorary Member of the Academy of Belles-Lettres of Barcelona.

1754 May 19: Died in Madrid.

PART I

Testimony of the Minor Works

CHAPTER 1

Personal History

IGNACIO de Luzán, who is best remembered as an exponent of Classical aesthetics, and who occupies in the history of Spanish literature a place similar to that of Boileau in France and Muratori in Italy, must have been in real life a person very difficult to know well. Despite the esteem with which he was regarded by intellectuals and by diplomatic and court authorities, almost nothing is known, on external evidence, about his human personality. For this there are probably three explanations. First, he appears to have been a scholar of a naturally retiring disposition and exclusive habits; one who would think cautiously before he spoke, whose inner reactions would be disciplined by external immobility. He was a type of scholar common enough in European life down to 1914: a type, not unrealistic, but selective in his associations with reality; a man withdrawn, and able, socially speaking, to remain withdrawn in the gentlemanly, professional seclusion of his own planned choice. Secondly, Luzán's whole life from his early orphaned years was one of dependence on the will of this or that uncle, of his elder brother, heir to the family estate; on the will, later, of persons in high society able to secure him a living suitable to his rank. In such circumstances a quiet, scholarly man does not, or did not, easily relax into naturalness, state his own opinions too forcefully, or demonstrate initiative inconvenient to his family and benefactors. Thirdly, the nature of one of his offices, as Assistant to the Spanish Ambassador in Paris, suggests that self-effacing diplomacy was both a quality of his mind and a feature of his career. If there is any small truth in the saying "like father like son," we have evidence of the same quality of modest discretion in the character of Luzán's son, Juan Ignacio, whose religious career, after his father's death, depended on the goodwill of benefactors. The elder Luzán, then, must have suppressed many inner thoughts when he spoke, as he suppressed them so often when he wrote. Where it is necessary for us to know him more intimately throughout the course of this study, we shall have to learn to analyze the quality of his silence and supply the context of his selectiveness.

The most detailed biography of Spain's best-known Preceptist was supplied by his son, Don Juan Ignacio Luzán, who for convenience may be referred to less confusingly hereafter as "Don Juan." This account was written to form an Introduction to the posthumous, second edition of Don Ignacio's chief work *La Poética,* or *Poetics,* published in 1789.[1] Here the reader is presented with all the necessary facts and circumstances of the elder Luzán's life. But Don Juan, struggling against his own ill health in 1789 to finish his task,[2] and, correct and discreet as his father before him, found little to say about other than external matters. All that occurred to him when he tried to sum up his father's character was that Don Ignacio was a shy, gentle scholar, whose life was free from vice, who entertained a sense of responsibility for the public good, yet whose very unassuming nature prevented him from reaching a position of material importance until almost the end of his life. This we can well believe. The tone of Don Ignacio's work invariably supports it.

As for the material facts supplied by the 1789 biography: Ignacio de Luzán Claramunt de Suelves y Gurrea, the youngest of several children, was born in Zaragoza, capital of the Spanish province of Aragon, on March 28, 1702. His parents, Antonio de Luzán y Guaro and Leonor Pérez Claramunt de Suelves y Gurrea, belonged to the upper class of landed gentry and lived on their estate in Zaragoza. This was a part of Spain with a strong sense of political independence and a long tradition of culture. Until the coming of the first Bourbon to the Spanish throne in 1700, Aragon, like Catalonia, had preserved many of its ancient laws and privileges; like Catalonia it had sided in the Spanish War of Succession with the Austrian Pretender; and, in the early decades of the eighteenth century it shared Catalan resentment at the loss of regional privileges and the necessity of subservience to the victorious French claimant occupying the throne in Madrid as Felipe V of Spain.

Don Antonio de Luzán, who had held the important post of Governor of the Province of Aragon, was evidently caught in the political turmoil of the Spanish War of Succession, being obliged to leave his home and move with his family to Barcelona where he died in 1706, nine years before the war ended. By this time Doña Leonor had also died and Ignacio was left in the care of his paternal grandmother, herself now elderly and ailing. So that the background of the boy's early childhood was one of political disturbance, war, reduced economic circumstances, orphanhood, and family sickness. As he grew older his books—given his studious nature—must have acted as a positive release from his personal deprivations.

We are told in the 1789 biography, that Ignacio's cultured parents had originally laid careful plans for his education, undoubtedly with highly capable tutors. But it was of necessity his grandmother who gave him his earliest instruction "in the true religion," "Christian and political virtues," and "who encouraged his affinity for knowledge." [3] However, after the siege of the city of Barcelona and the end of the War of Succession in 1715, Ignacio was sent to Mallorca to join Josef de Luzán, a clergyman uncle, who took him first to Genoa and later to Milan, where he was stationed for some five or six years.

From this time onwards Ignacio's studies progressed comprehensively and rapidly. His uncle placed him in a college for the children of the nobility, under the direction, Don Juan thought, of Jesuit Fathers, and there he quickly learned the Italian, French, and Latin which were to serve him so well in his future intellectual career. Apparently, like certain kinds of highly intelligent children whose early education, uncompetitive, and ruled by gentle old ladies, has been inferior to their capacities, he learned with unusual avidity and speed when given the stimulus of trained teachers; with, moreover, the greater modesty and stamina for knowing that he had so much to learn, and for having had to depend so much on his own resources. Among the serious books he had studied alone in Barcelona was the voluminous history of Spain by Juan de Mariana,[4] an indication both of the boy's historical propensities and of his disciplined patience.

I *Monstrous Curiosity*

The significant scene for the next, the most formative phase in Luzán's personal life, is Sicily, where Ignacio's guardian-uncle, Don Josef, had been made Inquisitor. The young student, journeying there with him, took advantage of an initially short stay in

Naples, on the way to Palermo, to study the *Logic* of Aristotle, and so to be introduced to models of schematization for which he later became famous.

This awakening of his interest in the Greek philosopher can hardly be overstressed. But what eventually mattered was not so much the fact that Luzán studied Aristotle, whom every student in every European university of the eighteenth century learned to know to some extent, as that he studied this ancient authority in enlightened Italy rather than in the then unenlightened Spain, and therefore learned to accept his prodigious authority in proper proportion. Had he studied Aristotle at that time in Spain, he would have been taught to accept him as the ultimate criterion for all techniques of thinking, whether ancient or modern, Spanish or Greek. But in Italy, as in England and France, Aristotle had become more open to criticism, and Luzán, ardent student though he was of the Greek Master, never assumed that Aristotle was in every respect infallible.

At about the same time, in the early twenties of the century, Ignacio, who appears to have inherited no independent income, was seriously considering his future, and being, his biographer tells us, of too "gentle a disposition" [5] for a military career, considered as one of the alternatives for younger sons, he chose a career in Law, eventually graduating as Doctor of Laws at the University of Catania in 1727.

Even in Law, however, he showed a strain of interior independence which makes his scholarship in any field arrestingly intelligent. Not content, says his son, with the prescribed course, he studied Law widely for himself. Likely enough he was inspired by the example of Giambattista Vico, a Professor of Law at the University of Naples, who was taking a more rational and scientific view of his subject than was usual, and who is one of the Italians quoted by Luzán. Not content, either, with one specialized branch of knowledge, he studied some of the subjects dear to the practical century: Modern Experimental Philosophy—we should call it Physics and Mathematics. He also learned German and Greek. For, so far, he had worked on Aristotle through Latin translations and his curiosity instinctively led him to original sources. To all of which he added Moral Theology, Literature, Music, and Drawing: a comprehensive education inspired, and in many cases directed, by tutors of the Jesuit Order which in Italy and France, as distinct from Spain, was just then in the forefront of intellectual advancement. It was this wide range of assiduous study, which provoked a friend to speak of Luzán's "monstrous curiosity" [6] and to fear for its effect on his health and sanity. Evidently the friend was not himself a serious intellectual. As Luzán tried to explain to him, concentrated and prolonged study does no harm to the man who is used to it and who is trained to organize his energies aright. By now Don Ignacio was writing poetry and working on treatises and translations. Now, too, he began to employ his leisure at meetings of intellectual societies, or Academies, where critical debate encouraged members to pursue new lines of thought. For instance, he became a member of a Palermo Academy which met in the house of the Prince of Santa Flavia. More significantly he attended an "Academy of Good Taste" which met in the house of an Italian scholar, Canon Panto, and undoubtedly helped to shape the principles of literary taste with which this method-loving, but open-minded Doctor of Laws was to become publicly associated.

When Don Josef, "at whose expense Ignacio lived," [7] died in 1729, the young man went back to Naples to live with his brother, Count Luzán, Governor at the time of the Castle of San Telmo. He seemed to have had no decisive inclination to enter the collegiate life of a university or religious order. Or it may be that his health was not considered equal to such professional requirements.[8] Had he lived nowadays he would perhaps have tried to earn his living by some kind of free-lance writing. But in noble families of his times, it must be remembered, dependence was a more honorable means of livelihood than would be the regular exercising of a career for monetary reward. Therefore, in Naples, the scholar continued in gentlemanly leisure to instruct himself, a little impeded, we hear, by "health" problems and consequently obliged for a time to study less and meditate more on what he knew already: a phase, as his son most rightly observes, valuable for the "deepening" as opposed to the extending of his knowledge.[9] In Naples he took full advantage of his opportunities for mixing with the cultured and erudite society resident there. It was a golden era of his intellectual development which lasted until 1733.

II *Reentry into Spanish life*

In this year Luzán went to Spain and entered the history of Spanish literature. Initially he had gone to Zaragoza, at his brother's request, to organize the administration of the family lands and property which had fallen into neglect, and he spent the next few years between the quiet Aragonese towns of Monzón and Huesca, places more conducive, Don Juan says, to his "philosophic and studious life" than Zaragoza itself.[10] During this time and with the Neapolitan background and his Italian-formed principles fresh in his solemn young mind, he prepared the final version of the work already written in Italy and by which he is best remembered: the *Poetics,* or a treatise on the rules and principles of good taste for poetry and drama. This he published in Zaragoza in 1737 with the obvious intention of giving to the new Spain of the new Bourbon enlightenment an equivalent to the French and Italian codes of art.

Meanwhile, we are told, he was looking for a wife, a quest which he seemed to plan as rationally as he planned the rest of his affairs. For her domestic usefulness seemed to be his predominant requirement, and there is no indication from external or internal evidence that his courting or his marriage affected the nature of his intellectual absorption. The prospective lady certainly does not seem to have appeared before his imagination as an intellectual companion. She was prosaically "to serve as a comfort in his by no means prosperous situation and to manage the domestic economy which gifted lovers of learning usually find irksome and unpractical." [11] Therefore he deliberately sought his future wife, not among the more sophisticated ladies of Zaragoza, but among the more domesticated, and, one suspects, the more docile ladies of the countryside. His calculated choice fell upon Doña María Francisca Mincholet, who came from a respected family of country gentry. It supposes a strangely cold approach to matrimony. But the rationalist is often obliged to go about nonrational matters in a rational manner, and there is something a little pathetic, perhaps, about this scholar's calculating diffidence. At least, however, Luzán did not include money among the attributes he required of a wife. Because now, finding the allowance provided by his brother too small for family needs, he began, shyly, and therefore for some time unsuccessfully, to seek employment in professional or political circles in Madrid by the only means then open to a gentleman, that is to say by means of recommendations and introductions to court officials.

Even, however, if the means were discomfiting to his quiet pride, his aim, we imagine, was a quietly proud bid for the personal freedom of monetary independence. Perhaps the practical lady Doña María encouraged him in his venture. At all events, there is no suggestion that the idea of suitable employment was anything but pleasurable to him and when, at length, he obtained it, he entered upon his work with interest and with a sense of eager responsibility.

III   *Official Recognition. Paris and Madrid*

During his stay in Madrid, Don Ignacio had become well known in intellectual circles and, by virtue of his *Poetics*, and of his Italian and French learning, he was soon recognized as a valuable ally in the cause of intellectual progress. By 1741 he had become an Honorary Member of the Royal Academy of the Spanish Language. In 1742 he was made a supernumerary of the same. A little later he was admitted to the newly founded Academy of History.

In fact, it was because his fame as a scholar had slowly but surely permeated the more intellectual reaches of government that he obtained his first employment. He was invited in 1747 to accept a post at the Secretariat of the Spanish Embassy in Paris under the Duke of Alba: a post hardly worthy of Don Ignacio's standing, thought Count Luzán, who possibly would have found it convenient to retain his brother in gentlemanly indigence administering his estate, yet a post which Don Ignacio himself "gladly welcomed." [12] Thus it happened that, by one of those apparent coincidences which are not coincidences at all but a predisposition for *like* instinctively to seek out *like*, Luzán went with his Classical culture and his scholarly objectivity to the Classical capital just at the historical juncture when its writers were in the process, not, certainly, of abandoning their Classical ways, but of modernizing and rationalizing them. The Spaniard's second edition of his *Poetics*, which he was revising in the late 'forties and early 'fifties, though it was never published in his lifetime, is a testimony to the fact that in harmony with the changing moods of France in particular and of Europe in general, he was bringing his own principles up to date also.

Don Ignacio remained in Paris from 1747 until May 1750, acting as Ambassador in the interval that elapsed between the retirement of the Duke of Alba and the appointment of his successor. All of which work was carried out to the satisfaction of the Madrid government, explains his son, "despite the delicate political situation" [13]—a reference presumably to tensions between Spain and France during 1747 and 1748, when these allies in the War of the Austrian Succession were not fully in accord over its termination and the provisions of the Treaty of Aix-la-Chapelle. On his return to Spain in May 1750, when he settled in Madrid, Luzán obtained offices which certainly indicate that his ability and discretion had been approved in high quarters. He was appointed to posts attached to the Treasury and Chamber of Commerce, was made Superintendent of the Royal Mint and Treasurer of the Royal Library, and was entrusted with various confidential government commissions.

In literary and academic quarters he also began to enjoy the prestige and respect which his standards of culture merited. He had published in 1751 his impressions of educational reform and literary culture in Paris. In 1751, too, he was received as a member of the exclusive Academy of Good Taste under the presidency of the Marchioness of Sarria. He was a founder-member of the Academy of San Fernando, opened by Fernando VI in 1752 for the development of the three noble Arts. In the same year he was made an Honorary Member of the Royal Academy of Belles-Lettres of Barcelona. Privately he continued to write poetry, to translate, and to project scholarly treatises, most of which remained unpublished or unfinished.

But those passing references to his health made by Don Juan from time to time and given small significance in the body of the biography must have represented preparatory murmurings of the serious disease, probably unsuspected as such, which became fatally acute in 1754. He died on May 19, 1754, just when the King had decided to appoint him "to one of the highest posts of the realm," [14] asserts Don Juan who goes on to supply indirect but convincing evidence on the subject. It is indeed noteworthy that the King made himself responsible for the scholar's family. He granted pensions to Luzán's wife and daughter, educated his two sons, and settled them in their respective professions.

Altogether one does not feel that Don Ignacio's work was finished in 1754. Sad as it may be that death prevented him from taking advantage of the eminent opportunities then being offered to him, it is even sadder that his interesting maturity should have been abruptly terminated precisely when he was turning it to practical account. It is saddest of all that the second edition of his *Poetics* was not edited by himself. A manuscript note by his friend Llaguno, a younger man of less talent and philosophical comprehension, asserts that some of the alterations and "observations" were made by Llaguno himself.[15] We believe that in Luzán's own independence, and the new broad-mindedness of his post-Paris experience, he would have produced a much more thoughtful version than did his editors, possibly the most rational and empirical of all modern *Poetics* to that date.

CHAPTER 2

Luzán the Academician

I *Academia de Buen Gusto (Academy of Good Taste)*

FEWER learned societies of distinction had been founded in
Spain than, for instance, in France, Italy, or England. Spain
had been less inclined, possibly for reasons of temperament, to put
her national faith in royal collegiate management. Like the English literary house parties—those of Mrs. Thrale or Horace Walpole—or like the casual literary gatherings in London taverns
and coffee houses, Spanish societies were usually informal groups
of individuals rather than organized associations. But the rapid
development of scientific experiment, and, in consequence, the
need for technical education were in Luzán's time attracting state
attention. The Royal Academy of the Spanish Language had been
instituted in 1713, the Royal Academy of Medicine and Surgery
in 1732, the Academy of History in 1735, and the Royal Academy
of Practical Jurisprudence in 1742. Others followed in Madrid
and the provinces. An increase in the number of smaller, private
societies, dedicated to the Arts and mindful of sophisticated
salons of France or Italy, was also largely the result of Bourbon
standards of values. It was to one of the most exclusive of these
private societies, the ambitious Academia de Buen Gusto (Academy of Good Taste),[1] that Luzán, already familiar with the
workings of learned and artistic Academies in Italy, was admitted
as a distinguished authority on poetry, a Spanish Dr. Johnson.
Since the Academy of Good Taste, in its private and literary emphasis, is so much more important for our general understanding
of Don Ignacio than the national Academy of History to which
he had been admitted earlier, and since space does not permit
us to accompany him to all the Academies of which he was a
member, we shall confine ourselves to observing him at work in
the *salon* of the Marchioness of Sarria.

By comparison with modern literary societies, the Academy

of Good Taste was astonishingly exacting. Though members met
in comfort in the noble rooms of the Marchioness,[2] duly partook
of the refreshments for which their hostess is duly thanked in the
Minutes of February 25, 1751, incidentally, perhaps half-idly,
read and discussed new works together, and doubtless indulged
for part of each session in general conversation, they were all
expected to work too, and to assume critical responsibilities. Their
purpose was not to be addressed by some visiting lecturer, poet,
or other important personage. At every meeting each member was
expected to make his own active contribution. In turn, each read
aloud some original composition on a subject either assigned to
him or of his own choosing. Again in turn, each acted as formal
judge and critic of his colleagues' work.

Despite the sketchiness of the handwritten Minutes, details
are recorded there about the democratic alternation of presiding
officers, about attendances, the subjects prescribed to each member for poetic treatment, and about admission of new members
under their pseudonyms.[3] Copies of members' poems usually accompany these notes, together with criticism which the poems had
provoked. The Marchioness herself is referred to as the President.
The Marquis, mentioned only once, on December 1, 1750 as a
witness of his wife's talented acting, is otherwise conspicuous in
the Minutes by his absence or anonymity. The Marchioness was
evidently a figurehead and seems not to have contributed poetry
herself, though it is difficult to believe that a cultured lady, ready
to lend her house or gardens and grace the solemn proceedings
so assiduously, could not have written verse at least as good as
that of the weakest poems to survive. But the general enthusiasm
at some periods was remarkable. Meetings continued into the
torrid heat of July and August when even the orchard-gardens
of noble mansions would be wilting with airlessness.[4]

The Marchioness' hardworking Academy was not all of one
mind either about poetry or poetic criticism. Certain members,
such as Porcel and the Conde de Torrepalma, expressed views
or shaped poems in accordance with Baroque tradition.[5] Their
models were the great Spanish masters, so that where debate
turned on French and Italian precepts and Classical ideals, these
members might be heard reasserting the free rights of genius.
Others, like Blas Antonio Nasarre who had edited Cervantes'
plays [6] and Agustín de Montiano, the dramatist,[7] followed French

practice and favored modernized Gallo-Classicism in the interests of modernized reasoning and scientific method. Nevertheless, so far as the evidence of the Minutes goes, controversies on these subjects were tolerant, members apparently conducting themselves like the gentlemen they were, at least before the Lady President. At the same time we should realize that Luzán, who in the first volume of the *Poetics* had disclosed singular ignorance of Spanish literature, yet who had always seemed receptive and fair-minded, must have been influenced and informed by discussions among intellectual Spaniards about their own brilliantly unique literature: by discussions between, for example, Porcel and Montiano, by arguments for and against national principles of literary independence. It is significant that the second, the posthumous edition of his *Poetics*, revised, all authorities insist, from his own notes left unfinished at the time of his death, is usually less narrow and much more Spanish in understanding than the first.

II *El Peregrino (The Wanderer)*

Luzán was admitted to this illustrious society of noblemen and noble intellects on July 16, 1750, when the Academy, according to the extant Minutes, had been meeting regularly for at least eight months. Following a coy practice inherited from the literary self-consciousness of Renaissance Italy, the members had adopted descriptive pseudonyms: The Drone, The Adventurer, The Humble One, The Satyr etc.: names which in general it could be misleading now to interpret categorically. A sophisticated company might enjoy calling its members by names suggesting the opposite qualities to those they really possessed, by names derived from a complicated association of ideas or personalities now lost, names derived from real characteristics, from deceptive appearances, names given now for one reason, now for another. Luzán's name, "El Peregrino," The Pilgrim or Wanderer, has, however, a special significance for the history of eighteenth-century literature and ideas. Here was an illustrious scholar whose background was crossed with foreign travel—of travel, moreover, in countries of Classical standards. Here was a representative of Preceptists who conceived it their business to maintain for modern reasons the Classical principles of order and harmony, avoiding the merely popular, the theoretically illogical, the Baroque exaggerations of the previous century; cooperating with the Bourbon ideal of organized authority and gracious discipline.

The Wanderer to most members of this Academy, and to Bourbon intellectuals elsewhere, was the Ambassador of Enlightenment at Spain's Court of Ignorance. Quite apart from the *Poetics,* his serious poem *El juicio de París (Judgment of Paris)* of 1746 was now known and would be recognized correctly as about the best and most modern-sounding poem the century had yet produced. Rightly or wrongly, too, Luzán was credited by the intelligentsia of the 'forties and early 'fifties with a practical vision of what the new Spanish culture ought to be. Certainly, whether by reason of his reputation or of his personality, he injected new life into the Academy of Good Taste. If the Minutes are accurate, attendances were falling when he was admitted. For some time previously, numbers of working members had varied from a mere four to five out of a possible eight or nine, or more. Of the most assiduous, only The Adventurer, Porcel, a not despicable imitator of the Milton-like Fernando de Herrera and, more commonly, a writer of popular verse, ever showed genuine imagination. The Joker, that is to say the pedantic Nasarre, was a singularly dull joker in print. The Humble One, the dramatist Montiano, was distressingly matter-of-fact, and the Drone, José Villarroel, was primarily a critic and not a very good one.

Further, the themes prescribed by the Academy for poetic treatment by its members, who might be described under the collective pseudonym of Poetic Inadequacy, were hardly calculated to bring out the best in their subartistic natures. Some poems were even put together compositely, each member assuming responsibility for one section, much as, nowadays, various aspects of a subject of investigation are distributed for consideration among the different members of a research team. One of their most persistent collective activities in this respect was a well-intentioned commentary on the Lord's Prayer which stretches and strains, as mercilessly exhaustive as it is characterless, over several academic sessions. Having started out on so pious a course, the members appeared to believe themselves in honor bound to persevere conscientiously to the last sacred word, and a reader has difficulty in determining which of their collective capacities, the religious or the poetic, comes off worse. From the poetic point of view, the Academy probably met too often. Doubtless, however, there were social reasons also for the frequency of its sessions.

But with the arrival of Luzán, the Academy, or rather its Minutes, spring into more constructive life. A record number of members were in attendance that day, and standing out in the files among the jaded expositions of the Lord's Prayer is a poem of enthusiastic welcome to that Wanderer who had come with the Parisian effluvia of Enlightenment swirling about his person. Of course the naturally courtly manners of Spaniards were exaggerated in the eighteenth century wherever public or semi-public occasions thrust them into prominence; and in this jocular verse-address, made with the solemnly academic wit which now we sometimes hear in formal presentations for Honorary Degrees, courtliness was made overconspicuous in the absence of poetic competence and artistic finesse. Therefore, we must not pay undue attention to the Academy's paean of praise, though it is worth noticing which of Luzán's qualities and which facts of his experience occur to the hymn-writer as being worthy of mention. The opening, "Most famous Luzán," is natural enough. The Academy saw the *Poetics* of 1737 as a manual of literary Good Taste and would regard its author as a man to venerate. An immediate reference to his stay in Paris is another indication of the Academy's sense of priorities. Luzán's nicety of speech is a virtue justifiably noticed only slightly later, and is one which any Academy of Good Taste might be expected to propagate. As irony would have it, however, the hymn extolling Luzán's anti-Baroque nature itself takes a disconcertingly Baroque turn with the florid description of Don Ignacio's writings as "ruby words on diamond pages." Which tribute, representing all the fancy fatuousness that the Wanderer hoped to reform, must have made him, and possibly his fellow model of exquisite nicety, Montiano, inwardly wince and despair.

The rest of the poem of welcome asks disingenuous questions about Paris which are meant as witticisms, but which emerge as inanities. "Is there still a Round Table?" "Is there public freedom of conscience . . ?" In fact, were this the limit of the poet's inquiry, one might dismiss him, together with his colleagues, as unrewarding dilettanti. However, the casual mention, in a slightly different context about historical authenticity, of the name Feijoo, Spain's most realistic thinker of the period, suggests, as we might have anticipated from the personnel, that the Academy's reading was enterprising, and that this society, like the other learned societies to which Luzán belonged, was receptive to the manifestations of scientific change. A man's associates of like mind do not invariably explain him to us. Often he relaxes best in the company of opposites. Yet if the persons whose company he voluntarily chooses to frequent at one stage of his life are similar in mentality to those with whom he associates at other stages, then such companions can tell us much about his own ways of thought.

It would be misleading to draw precise conclusions from the sketchy, incomplete Minutes of the Academy of Good Taste. The clear fact remains, however, that no sooner had Luzán been admitted to its membership than the critical spirit quickened, in response, apparently, rather than in opposition to his presence, just as critical inquiry quickened in London coffeehouses and drawing rooms whenever Dr. Johnson entered them. Evidently the mere presence of an acknowledged authority is itself a challenge to the intellect of his companions, particularly on easily understandable and controversial matters. Additionally too, perhaps, the Secretary of the Academy of Good Taste, Montiano, whose casualness so far is what might be expected from men who put original composition first and administration second, was inspired by the heightening of critical atmosphere to preserve the Academy's formal critiques during the next few sessions. For although the Academy, apparently from its beginning, had boasted a series of critics or "Judges" of its own work, their judgments had remained unrecorded. We must, repeat, however, that the extant, fragmentary Minutes may do less than justice to Academy administration.

III *The Critic Criticized*

Aware as he must have been of this heightened atmosphere of criticism, Don Luis Velázquez, The Seaman, who had the honor to follow Luzán into the Academy, produced as his discourse of admission, seemingly under the direction of the Academy, a paper in prose on the qualities necessary to a poet.[8] Evidently the presence of the Wanderer had directed the mind of the Marchioness' salon on a new course, for it is not until now that the Minutes record urgent investigation into the nature of poetry.

Here Luzán, then, knowingly or not, appears to have stimulated an inquiry into artistic essentials that parallels inquiries, in other intellectual societies, into the essential nature of physical man and the physical world he inhabits. Poetry had been characterized by authorities ancient and modern now in one way, now in another. Those ways had not always coincided. Sublime practice had not always conformed to theoretic ideals. What then, was poetry? In fact, what was sublimity? What was definable man that he could possess indefinable attributes? Rationalism, which for some time had plagued the minds of the practical scientists, was now plaguing the consciousness of men of letters.

The Seaman was not equal to this momentous occasion. Even if the majority of his listeners were at that time impressed—he tried, seemingly, to cater for all tastes—the newly admitted Wanderer must have smiled to himself as he heard his latest colleague floundering in a muddle of self-contradictory plagiarisms, the only clear thought among which was that a poet, to be sublime, must have sublime genius. Luzán had already organized the subject better, quoting his authorities correctly, in the *Poetics* of 1737. He would know that the question of whether sublimity is or is not acquirable had been debated coherently by, for example, Muratori,[9] and that many of the rules being ponderously prescribed by the Seaman for the avoidance of poetic defects and the acquisition of poetic virtues were unconscious travesties of Luzán's rules elegantly codified in the *Poetics*. Doubtless he would also know that various phrases used to describe the qualities of a genius able successfully to transcend rules—"a certain mental knack" or "freedom of spirit"—together with the arguments that rules and study cannot make even a mediocre poet, that beauty does not consist in geometric proportions, but in a certain "combination of fortuitous circumstances," were not the Seaman's own words, but borrowed from Feijoo whom the century regularly quoted, wholly or slightly out of context.[10]

Nevertheless, the fact that Velázquez had ventilated Spanish doubts on the Preceptists' rights to confine genius, that even in the depths of his muddle, he had attempted to analyze rationally, further, the fact that in the following session the more imaginative and incisive Porcel defended the triumphs of the unconventional writers of Spain's Golden Age, of which Luzán knew so little, all this must have encouraged the receptive Wanderer to take

new evidence into new account. Luzán may not always have been well informed, least of all on literary styles which diverged from the French and Italian Classical norm. But, as his *Memoirs of Paris* shows, he had an honest mind, was prepared to reconsider all evidence, old and new, and to shift his position accordingly. This is one of the many occasions when we realize forcefully that had he lived long enough himself to complete the revision of his *Poetics*, he would assuredly have taken into account reputable works and points of view that he had not considered previously.

At the meeting on October 1, 1750, with eight working members present, a much livelier and more imaginative critique was presented by the appropriately named Adventurer, again in response to Luzán's ideas and practice, but this time directly. The "censure" uses a fictitious frame-dream in which the Adventurer flies to the moon to visit the Academy of the world's immortals and convey back to earth the judgment given by Spain's Golden Age masters on the Academy's poems. This judgment is described in the Minutes as "erudite and discreet," the second quality of which is, for our purposes, the more important of the two. For the *Juicio lunático*, or moon-critique, reveals an atmosphere of give-and-take which, on principle, evidently pervaded the Marchioness' drawing room also, and further shows how these enlightened men of reason were teaching themselves both to agree to disagree, and, whether agreeing or disagreeing, to behave with respectful tolerance. It was the formidable custom at the Academy of Good Taste for a judge, chosen from the members in turn, to pass critical commentary on the compositions of all the members. Recently in Spain there had been trenchant censure from Feijoo, among others, of the habit of allowing inane eulogy to pass for critical judgment.[11] Now the stern, hard-working gentlemen of this new Academy, possessed by the scientific spirit of inquiry, and, having steeled themselves to try to learn to be honest critics, were patently enjoying the exclusive sensation of their own objectivity. Incidentally, it might be noted that the Academy, like characters in the *Judgment of Paris*, could not let scientific subjects alone, and Porcel, at the outset, unnecessarily remarks on modern findings of Physics which had disproved Aristotelian ideas about the nature of the planets. The idea of the lunar Academy itself was probably as much inspired by current talk about the surface of the moon [12] as by literary fantasies of the past. Perhaps it was the single-mindedness of their serious purpose that had attracted Don Ignacio to these gentlemen of good taste.

The Adventurer's stimulating performance of his uncomfortable Fiscal-task, however, was largely due to his imaginative sensibility. He spared nobody, least of all Luzán. Yet the members would not have had to brace themselves unduly to accept his censure. In the best national tradition, he is disarming. When an intelligent Spaniard deliberately sets himself the task of expressing unpleasant truths tactfully, he can probably perform this task more acceptably than members of any other race in the world. The Adventurer is careful in each case to begin with praise for what can constructively be praised—there is always something praiseworthy, he observes with satisfaction—and he fairly censures defects which would be regarded as defects by good critics of any period. If some criticisms rankled, as doubtless they would in mere mortals, it was evidently the custom to accept them philosophically. The Minutes show no evidence of members resigning in a huff. On the contrary, they suggest that practice in critical analysis directed Academicians towards that state of open-mindedness for which the eighteenth century is so rightly respected.

Only Luzán of the Adventurer's willing victims need concern us. On the credit side, the Wanderer is found to observe poetic precepts with "such naturalness that they appear to have been made not for him but by him," so that where art is manipulated by him it "looks as if it has become part of nature," whereas in inferior hands it would fail to convince. This is a true judgment indeed. Luzán's whole strength was in his technique. But some small and inconspicuous examples of "carelessness" are noted, nevertheless, some faulty lines of reasoning, certain inappropriate phrases. Further, one of the immortals is moved disingenuously to remark that "excessive subjection to rules is as bad as absolute liberty." But it is only after all members have been passed under review, encouraged, and in some way found wanting, that the Adventurer—speaking through the mouth of the moon-raised Garcilaso—reaches his climax with a description of genius as a free agent, as the winged horse Pegasus, unbridled and out of reach. Then, having already dismissed the man-made rules of art as "overrated," at least where poetic masters are concerned, he winds up his judgment by vigorously asserting that a system of "Poetics" is merely an expression of "opinion." [13] It should be said at this point that, when making provision for his journey to the moon, and when the Adventurer had, he said, been advised to carry a volume of poetry to act as his amulet, he had chosen the poems of that *bête noire* of all Preceptists, Italian, French, or Spanish, the outrageously exaggerated but inimitable poet of the Spanish Baroque, the "Blessed" Luis de Góngora. Obviously this Fiscal demanded no immutable laws other than those of proportion, harmony and, as indeed he says in so many words, discriminating originality. Obviously too, the revered Luzán had entered this democratic Academy with none of the privileges fawningly assigned to dictator-Johnsons or Voltaires in hushed drawing rooms and coffeehouses. He went to learn, not to dictate; and his assiduous attendance and verse-practice there must mean that he had no objection to being instructed in the means of broadening his mind. On the one occasion when Luzán was obliged to miss a meeting in order to nurse a cold, he evidenced his regrets by forwarding his own homework in the shape of a sonnet, as sick but as punctilious as he.[14] For the formative Academy, once again we must realize, looked upon itself much more seriously than we might suppose, and was taken with full seriousness by the Wanderer.

A later set of Minutes in which Luzán's work and his Classical principles are reported as having been under review is one of the last: that of February 25, 1751. His critic now was a man of national Spanish sympathies, José Villarroel, The Drone, whose Judgment, if taken out of its context, undeniably sounds censorious to the point of viciousness. "Fancy," the Drone says in effect, "fancy thinking of dictating to the Muses, of giving them minute rules for the whys, the wherefores, the whens, the whats, the hows," for all the negative means of avoiding extravagance. It is all very right and proper, he goes on, turning now directly to the Academy's Preceptist, to expect a poet to try to write with ordinary care and correctness, but beyond that, any exercise of writing to rules is an exercise designed for children only. The Wanderer's attitude to poetry is not that of an eagle, but of an owl, and had his verse been judged by the great poets of Spain's past, it would have been rejected out of hand.

Within the Academy's context, however, these strictures

[33]

ring less offensively. First, it is clear from the brisk, popular air of the Drone's verse-judgment either that he was amiably accepted as, and took himself for the Society's licensed buffoon, or that, just as the Adventurer had used moon-fiction, he himself was using jocular impertinence as a conveniently general vehicle for criticizing all his friends. His lines are jaunty to the point of near-slang, giving the impression that his inadequacy—certainly he was not one of the outstanding writers of the group—rather than his intention made him express himself in bad taste. Secondly, all members are treated alike. The versification of the Classical tragedy *Virginia,* written by Montiano, The Humble One, and which Spain's intellectuals of the time regarded with pride, is described by the Drone as "turning my stomach." The Duke of Béjar, The Satyr, is censured for allowing his courtly muse to write like a rustic. Nasarre is found to parade too much lawyer-like erudition. The Count of Torrepalma, The Difficult One, is "finicky" and "pretty-pretty." The Andalusian Seaman is caricatured for his regionalistic pronunciation, and the Adventurer is told that he writes too much too boringly. Finally, the Drone, in the give-and-take spirit of the Academy, criticizes his own work with a splutter of disparagement.

It is true that the Wanderer comes in for rather more attention than the rest. That was natural enough. Artistically and intellectually he was one of the most eminent among them, and probably this Drone to whom the Spanish masters were sacred, disliked the Wanderer's emphasis on foreign values. Even so, when all these circumstances are taken into account, Villarroel's crudities are more clownish than malicious and, in their context, suggest that he enjoyed teasing as much as the members enjoyed being teased. There is a "family" atmosphere about his comfortable amusement and his cozy assumption of being accepted. Consequently, when Luzán left the Marchioness' house that day, he is unlikely to have gone with black anger clutching at his heart. Rather he would go, one must suppose, remembering how he had laughed with his friends, proud and pleased to have his famous literary foibles caricatured sympathetically. Friends laugh at each other's idiosyncrasies. At worst, the atmosphere must have been one of playful disagreement. And that, too, must have been very good for the Wanderer's owlishness.

After this date, the Academy Minutes become disorganized and

begin to fade quietly away. The translation of a Sapphic ode
by Luzán, read, perhaps, on April 29, 1751, is, for him, unusually
forced and clumsy. There is a sober account of the death of
Nasarre. It is very likely that the life went out of the Academy
with the onset of Luzán's own illness which led to his death a few
years later. He seems to have completed no new work after 1751.[15]

IV *Luzán the Poet*

By standards of artistic achievement, Luzán is disappointing.
Yet he disappoints interestingly, because, in nearly succeeding, he
inevitably exposes the strain on the inner mechanism of his
effort and, by such negative processes, illuminates the problem
of what constitutes genius. Moreover, his verse is worth acknowledgment for more positive reasons. It reminds us, for instance,
that when writing his theoretical *Poetics* he was drawing on
practical experience, on an inveterate habit indulged from boy-
hood onwards, of verse-making, and that in consequence he often
wrote the more understandingly for having inside knowledge. The
Poetics is a singularly practical treatise. More positively still,
where the human pulse of the eighteenth century can be detected
beneath his lyrical sophistication, it records gratifyingly casual
evidence of the epoch's thought-trend. Indeed the more conventional the poetic occasion, the more significant is any increase
in the pulse rate of a poet's perception.

Luzán's son was sufficiently aware of the dominating mountain
ranges of genius extensively crossing Spain's past to realize that
it would be absurd to stress such "gifts" as his father displayed on
the humble flats of the eighteenth century. In nearly all his poems,
Don Juan diffidently said, taking his cue from an anthologist of
the late 'sixties, López de Sedano, "there is more art than inspiration." Which does not mean, he qualified in some difficulty,
"that inspiration is altogether lacking." [16] Since Sedano had included a variety of Luzán's poems, to the exclusion of other
eighteenth-century works, in his *Parnaso español (The Spanish
Parnassus)*,[17] an anthology representing the artistic might of
Spain, it must be inferred that, by his standards also, inspiration
"was not entirely lacking" in the poetry of the Preceptist. "Inspiration," then, in some unspecified degree, was thought to be
there. But Don Juan, whose ill health may have deterred him
from dallying in troublesome subtleties, was unable to explain

this vital reservation. We think, he therefore suggested, with the helplessness of one anxious to finish his work while precarious health lasted, that the poet's outstanding quality was his "exquisite delicacy." [18]

The quality of "inspiration" which eluded these gentlemen may perhaps be said to consist of three special ingredients. First, though Luzán normally used conventional themes, he sometimes introduced into them current preoccupations like compulsive wonder at scientific progress. His "El Juicio de Paris," "Judgment of Paris," for instance, pauses in amazement on its semilaureate way of occasion to assimilate the new idea that everything living derives from egg cells, seeds within seeds, an infinity of realistic possibilities. Here "inspiration," glinting momentarily, is concerned with Luzán's desire to communicate a realistic interest which is obliged to act under its own stimulus. It constitutes a spark of personal vitality. In other moods he displays, too, a related talent for summarizing old thoughts, suddenly grown meaningful to his experience, in pithy new words.

Secondly, this poet whose technical competence gave him flexibility of movement, was also imaginative enough to conceive of lively images that paint scenes and strike sounds at one and the same time: like for example, "The startled shadows murmured in complaint" from his *Judgment of Paris*.[19]

Thirdly, in his burlesque of his own *Judgment of Paris*,[20] Luzán employs a quiet irony that takes us unawares. This is partly dependent on the use of comic repetition, a delicate sense of bathos, and an ability to dramatize the scene. But more important is his general tone of relaxed playfulness which proves that Don Ignacio could enter into the spirit of comedy and suggests that his highest creative potentiality was for modern comic drama.

CHAPTER 3

Memorias literarias de Paris
(Paris Memoirs)[1]

I *Literary Commerce*

COMPARED with the zestful travel diaries and journals in which the eighteenth century, dedicated to the study of man in his natural environment, reveled and excelled, Luzán's Paris *Memoirs* of 1751 seem strangely flat. It was not that he lacked curiosity, not even that he was unobservant. Nor would indifferent health fully account for the tonelessness of parts of his *Memoirs*. Some of the best autobiographical matter of the century was written by chronically sick men: Boswell and Cowper, Horace Walpole, Rousseau. . . . The explanation of Luzán's voice in Paris, bereft of resonance and the vibration of direct enthusiasm, a voice without the echoing confirmation of personal involvement, is probably as complicated as it is historically valuable. His is a cautious, noncommittal voice, telling of the state of mind of a whole class of eighteenth-century thinkers: the intelligent conservatives who shared a liberal interest in the international flow of literary ideas, who had grasped the meaning of the essentials of change, but who preferred to avoid or temporarily evade the realistic impact of the change in their everyday life. Luzán's observation is deliberately selective and his interpretation calculatedly shallow.

Historically speaking, this attitude, never specifically explained by Luzán for what it is, is an individual sign of the century's general posture of tension. Not every observant intellectual wanted to go along the whole of the rationalistic way in case it led to disturbing incomprehensibilities. Feijoos formed a very small minority. It was much commoner for intelligent scholars to make reservations, or, like Don Ignacio himself, to restrict their mental activities within known bounds. This certainly makes dryer and more inhibited men of them than the Feijoos who met life fully, face to face, ready to dare much and then to accept the mental consequences. Yet it shows that history must take into account men's natural retractions, negations, diffidence, and uncommitment, and reminds us that no century can be described simply in terms of progressives and reactionaries. Don Ignacio emerges from his *Paris Memoirs* as an observer who had planned what he was interested to observe, but who had extended his observations a little farther than he had originally arranged with himself; who was somewhat disconcerted by much of what he saw, but who did not want to disturb the reader or himself unduly by pursuing the implications of his disconcertedness.

It must be observed that his program was planned originally along nonpopular lines. He disliked, on principle, the use of "travelers' tales" for serious purposes and criticized them as weak sources in the otherwise weighty system of Montesquieu's *De l'Esprit des Lois (Concerning The Spirit of Laws).*[2] He was not interested in the way of life of the ordinary Frenchman. He wanted to see famous French writers hard at work, to tread the literary salons of the cultured, and make notes on the administration of great academies—in general, to follow abroad the cultural pursuits, literature, history, literary philosophy, in which he had been trained and which he could best understand. In the context of his diplomatic career, his progress was a kind of state progress, similar to that of a distinguished modern scholar on a world lecture tour who stays at embassies or official institutions, depends on academic recommendations, necessarily meets representative nationals with strict selectivity. So that Luzán's stay in Paris was vastly different physically and mentally from that of roving diarists who had the leisure and independence to wander off the official tracks and catch a country and its habits in unguarded moments. It may be that Luzán's Scholastic training, with its rigidly meticulous systematization of different forms of knowledge, caused him, despite his awareness of the need for educational reform, to confine his thoughts and themes within pre-prepared compartments; to leave him unable to assimilate and assess intuitively the more intangible French ideas which just then were massing outside the limits of the traditionally definable. At all events, the *Memoirs* omit mention of purely social and personal realities. Luzán's reports avoid not only the expected scenes and everday customs, but expected accounts and assessments of conversations, of personal visits to celebrities. Only exceptionally does he speak of private visits to institutions in which he was known to be interested. He makes no comment on the social behavior of the upper and upper-middle classes with whom he mixed, though he must have observed their behavior very closely, for he recognized it in its un-Spanish, un-Italian manifestations in La Chaussée's *Le Préjugé à la mode (The Man of Modish Taboos)*, which he translated with lively insight.[3]

Yet, in a broad sense, Luzán's aim was a reasonable one for the Age of Reason. He wanted to look for the causes of one certain effect. He wanted to find out for himself how it was that France had managed to make such conspicuous progress in what Spain understood as "Enlightenment," that is to say, in the development of all branches of knowledge under state protection, of educational reform, and of social administration. It should be observed, incidentally, that the *Memoirs* are dedicated to a notable Jesuit, Father Francisco de Ravago, the King's Confessor. This fact is triply significant. First, it proclaims the ultimate orthodoxy of Luzán's potential conclusions which indeed was never called into question. Secondly, in the context of Luzán's interest in educational reform along French lines, it testifies to the enlightenment of King and Confessor alike, and emphasizes the social broad-mindedness of which this king, Fernando VI, gave public proof, and for which the Jesuit Order, especially in France, was becoming a very respectable model. Thirdly, it places Fernando VI's influential Confessor in the position of supporting that state patronage of literature and educational reform desired not by Luzán only, but by the whole group of outward-looking intellectuals which he represented.

Dedication and official Approbation duly completed, Luzán is presented in print by his literary sponsor Montiano y Luyando, a colleague from the Academy of Good Taste, who shared Luzán's desire to reform the Spanish stage on Classical patterns and who practised in his tragedies what Luzán had preached in the *Poetics*.[4] Montiano too, it should be noted, held high office in the service of that Prince of Enlightenment Fernando VI, as a member of his Council. Wherefore, in approving Luzán's "original" curiosity and his useful observations, Montiano is speaking to some extent with state interests in mind. On a more personal level, he refers to Luzán's "modesty": an attribute we might do well to remember, for doubtless it often caused Don Ignacio to express what must have been strong feelings or anxieties in a decorously diffident way. One could have wished that the reserved Aragonese had been more self-revealing. But the unassuming nature of his scholarliness was genuine, and he always wrote in character. Accordingly, to his unobtrusive, understating, yet quietly perspicacious qualities, we must adapt any interpretation of his remarks.

Don Ignacio had approached one of the most cultured and brilliant capitals of Europe, "center of the sciences and the Arts, Belles-Lettres, erudition, delicacy, and good taste," [5] with his mind predisposed to admiration and with his steps unswervingly directed to the educational and cultural departments. Curiously enough, the personality of Paris as a city-individual seems to have made no impact on him. His description of the whole phenomenon of Paris reads like an arid paragraph from a guidebook and is confined to three and a half small pages. Yet here, on his first visit to Paris, was a historian whose intellect, one might suppose, would have strayed along the ancient ways of the French capital with a little more than casual interest. It is very noticeable that Luzán depends more on the indirect accounts of books and informants than he does on direct observation. Part of his *Memoirs* could have been written before he ever set foot in France. He writes with greater interest, even to the point of fussing over his statistics, about the annual consumption of foodstuffs in Paris than he does about that city's individuality. Evidently he was working to a program of logic designed for his research requirements exclusively: that is, for the study of the country's intellectual prosperity and social "Enlightenment." From his project, then, he was not disposed to swerve. Nor must we dismiss his attitude and method as peculiar to the obscure ways of life and thought of the past. It is, in fact, typical of the average scholar of any century. When the dedicated scholar sets out to investigate a situation in his particular field, he can usually resist the temptation of following temporarily alluring bypaths. His training in concentration has developed his self-defensive mechanism which conserves his energy and determines the best use of his time. The most readable journals, memoirs, diaries, and letters have seldom been those of dedicated scholars.

Besides, it will be remembered that Don Ignacio was evidently, by temperament, a man whose instinct was rather to judge the harmonized reason of books and bookish company than the raw material of which nature, man, and society are made. His initiative is not to be found in the search for the unknown, but in the organization of what has already been found or what he is mentally prepared to encounter.

II *The Spirit of Change*

Accordingly Luzán, moving through Parisian areas that serve his sophisticated purpose, visiting intellectual places recommended by French and foreign intelligentsia, comes to the first important observation of his visit: the inescapable fact that science is dominating the modern intellectual scene. In all intellectual quarters of this wider world beyond the Pyrenees, in every language, "speaking and writing follow scientific techniques." [6] Countless machines, countless instruments, are placed at the service of scholarship, he continues, in the tone of barely suppressed excitement that characterizes the speech of Intellect in the *Judgment of Paris* already discussed.

A dedicated man of letters like Luzán who had no practical interest in the sciences intrinsically and who was, moreover, a confirmed authoritarian, might almost have been expected to allow a note of forlornness to sound through his report on the domination of ideas by science. He might have been expected to shrink a little from those new machines and to shiver in the French fever of practical experiment. The fact that he does not is an enlightening indication of how the scholar-mind is normally obliged to function. It shows that where Luzán had planned to concentrate his informed attention he was objectively observant and openminded. It shows that elsewhere he was restrained in outlook and cautious in speech. It shows that he did not positively relate scientific activity to the human problems of mental reorientation which the acceptance of scientific evidence involved for those with minds realistic and independent enough to visualize all implications. He could enter into the general spirit of scientific progress while it remained diffused as a general atmosphere, because he had general confidence in the general superiority of France. But, as we shall see presently, he was not prepared to assess the far-reaching results of specific experiments. Perhaps too, like many traditionalists, he had a talent for not seeing what he did not want to see. So the panorama of scientific revolution, which fascinated or tormented greater men, was, to him, partially beclouded by his own preoccupations.

Before examining particulars of scientific disturbance, he begins, in his second chapter, and with an air of coming now to essentials, to introduce a series of technical items of information geared to the interests of educationists at home. These are continued to the end of Chapter 7. The details need not concern us. But it should be said that they are highly practical and are related to methods of teaching children from primary to senior grades. On such matters the Spanish scholar is knowledgeable and can fully recognize the value of modern French deviations from the traditional norm. It is true that again he appears to have consulted programs more than he has visited schools. But educational programs, in any case, are always modified, for better or for worse, by the personality of the individual teacher.

More essential to the present purpose is Luzán's knowledge of influential European educationists. Even if he had not mentioned the Englishman John Locke specifically by name, we should have known of his presence somewhere in Luzán's Franco-Italian consciousness. Evidently he knew Locke at second hand for he did not appear to recognize as Locke's the many educational theories which enterprising Parisians were busily putting into practice and which were soon to be adapted and elaborated by J. J. Rousseau. Luzán knew, he said, that the learned John Locke had written an excellent work on the Education of Children, a phrase which apparently he takes to be Locke's title. The work concerned must be the treatise *Some Thoughts Concerning Education* of 1693. This direct reference to the Englishman is solely on the grounds of Luzán's preference for private over public education.

But the teaching of Locke is inherent in most of the theories on child treatment which Luzán catches like an infection from Locke's French disciples: for instance, the principle, new at least in detail, that children are rational beings; that they should be encouraged to ask questions, should be given reasonable answers, and should as far as possible be treated as equals. Therefore

Luzán approves the French custom of addressing schoolchildren by the formal pronoun *vous,* the *you,* previously reserved for equals and superiors, rather than the *tu* suggesting inferiority, and he wishes the same practice were possible in Spain. Though here again he shows that his knowledge of Spanish was logical rather than practical, for the Spaniards' use of the informal *tú* had more to do with intimacy than inferiority. Perhaps the French determination to banish class distinction among pronouns was itself due to the precedent set by the gradual fading of the English "thou," a dangerously idiomatic pronoun too. Another tenet of John Locke, probably unrecognized as such, but which Luzán noted with special approval among the new French theories of education, was the condemnation of severity, impatience, shouting, and unkemptness on the part of teachers. For those of tender age are as of wax, protests Luzán, using, albeit unknowingly, Locke's very words,[7] and how can severity train them in human understanding, courtesy, confidence, and freedom from constraint? Further he supports, rather surprisingly for a man of his conservative training, the extension of higher education to women. Of course there were famous French women scholars moving on high levels of society. He instances, among others, the Marquise du Châtelet, celebrated for her grasp of Newtonian science. He would be aware, too, of the robust good sense of Feijoo [8] on the same subject. He knew that the Spanish Juan Luis Vives, a tutor of Mary Tudor, had held enlightened views on the academic potentialities of female mentality and he wished that Vives' treatise on this theme had been translated and become more widely known.[9] At the same time, in his personal commentary on the same question, Luzán is clearly taking into consideration the unexpressed fear felt even by advanced intellectuals that woman, given a man's education, might rise to challenge man's authority. It was a fear that many scholars, not liking to admit to it openly, had transmuted into a set of principles defining the sacred ideal of womanliness. It was a natural fear of an unassessable potentiality. Woman was enigmatic and traditionally her emotional power, the only power she had regularly exercised, was intimidating.

Luzán, however, had not only met famous French women intellectuals and knew them to be very different from those bluestocking figures-of-fun in Molière's *Les femmes savantes,* but, by the time he had completed his *Memoirs,* he knew and revered a gracious Spanish hostess, intelligently dispensing literary patronage in a seemly Spanish setting, the Marchioness of Sarria whom we met in the last chapter. Also he knew enough of Parisian society from the inside to be able to correct the non-French public in its assumption that Parisians were as regardless of decorum as foreigners vaguely supposed. His judgment on this subject is one of the most penetrating and rational judgments of the *Memoirs* and shows that, where he was interested to observe, he could observe with judicial understanding.

III *Literary Crisis*

Predictably, Don Ignacio is at his most expansive in speaking of the literature, the literary personages, and the literary institutions of Enlightened France. Some of his most practical notes record details of constitutions of such Societies and Academies as he hoped to see established or developed in an Enlightened Spain. He evinces special interest in the French Academy, the Academy of Belles-Lettres, and the illustrious histories of both. But he supplies conscientious information, particularly from Chapter XVI onwards, on the progressive Academies of Surgery, Sciences, Painting, Sculpture, and Architecture, as well as on Botanical Gardens, Military Schools, and the Sorbonne. He tells us next to nothing about the materials with which these Societies worked. Probably he would have understood very little about them. His main concern was the administrative policy of the Societies and the example they set to modern governments.

Even so, it is a little surprising to hear him approvingly making free of the name of Voltaire. Certainly Voltaire was one of the idols of the Enlightened, and Luzán's intellectual circle, described round the throne, recognized Voltaire's true worth. But in Spanish Church circles to which Luzán also intimately belonged, Voltaire's name by 1751 was already suspect and his works were soon to figure on the Index.[10] Don Ignacio, then, if respectfully mindful of Church authorities, was evidently not timorous. It should be remembered, however, that the name of Voltaire was less sinister to Spain in 1751 than it would be after 1789 when it came to be connected with the movement which had dethroned the French Bourbons and which caused Spain, under her own

Bourbon king, to tighten censorship as a safeguard against proletariat infection.

Although Luzán goes out of his way cautiously to praise Voltaire as "able . . . subtle . . . a scholar of lively imagination . . ."[11] and to describe him as the victim of envy and malicious criticism, his own interest in the Frenchman is primarily literary and largely related to his poems and plays. Yet the dramas he singles out for special mention, *Zaïre* and *Nanine,* are plays of modern social theses and so introduce a conversational relevance to modern life, of which the Spanish theater was sorely in need. *Nanine,* he reminds his readers, is based on an English novel, and it is designed, he says with deliberateness, to prove the ideal of "the equality of all men and the right to be distinguished by merit alone."[12]

Later in the century, this sentiment would have been considered dangerous. Where bandied about in Spain during the French Revolution, in certain popular plays for example, it was sometimes regarded by the censor as provocative.[13] Even in 1751 Luzán did not care to enlarge on such a theme. And that was not the only occasion when he stated the principles of the notoriously "enlightened" and left them without direction from himself to settle where they would.

Another important example of the same indirectness is his uncommentated quotation from Maupertuis whose new system of Metaphysics he approved. This author had asserted that Scholastic Metaphysics, the Metaphysics of Aristotle, was an *"inhospitable soil, productive only of weeds and thorns"*—the italics are Luzán's —and which had been used and survived merely because no other was known.[14] Indirect methods can be forceful, and consequently were forcefully used by many guarded intellectuals writing for a Spanish public. Where Luzán, or anybody in a similar position, used such force vicariously, it may be assumed that he did not disapprove of the general principle or sentiment quoted, at least as a philosophical proposition. For it is equally evident that wherever he disapproved of advanced ideas, on either religious or moral grounds, he had no hesitation, as we shall see later, in condemning them.

Here the psychology of his reasoning is obvious. His attention revolved round modern social drama, but for somewhat different reasons from those which were inspiring Voltaire and La Chaussée. French social drama employed a provocative thesis and, in the context of eighteenth-century French politics, belonged not only to artistic spheres but acted as popaganda in a new democracy of ideas for which England, in politics and modern social literature, was an insinuating model.[15] If Luzán knew this, which is unlikely, for as a threat it would be less evident to rationalism than to intuition, he certainly betrays no hint of such knowledge in his praise of French drama. Those social themes, which he appears not to see as political obsessions, are regarded by him from the standpoint of reasonable social reform as understood by enlightened Spanish Bourbons, or from that of literary originality. In the first case, he would agree with enlightened Spanish intellectuals that it was no disgrace for a gentleman to have dealings with supposedly sordid commerce and trade, and that any society finding shame in honest work was an anachronism. Theoretically he would approve the logic that a man's honor is more concerned with his inner character than with his outer status. On the literary side Luzán, in his rational moderation, was drawn to the verisimilitude or what the eighteenth century considered to be verisimilitude of that new, French, half-way drama between Classical tragedy and comedy: a play in which middle-class citizens faced unpretentious tragedies and lifelike sentiments; a play in which the problems of commoners lent themselves to natural interpretation by the common-judgment of audiences; a play narrowly confining its activities to selective tensions in family circles and observing the Unities out of psychological necessity. Not lightly or casually, therefore, did Luzán exercise himself in transposing the ordinary human tensions of La Chaussée's *Man of Modish Taboos* into *Reason versus Convention*.[16] Not merely casual, either, was his interest in the dramatic experiments of Voltaire.

By 1751 Luzán had mellowed. His conception of verisimilitude had deepened and extended. He had come to realize that new forms of drama might be more satisfyingly verisimilar to a rational age than the old. His inexperienced rigidity over Classical rules of form and expression had also considerably relaxed. His *Memoirs* still present him as a custodian of the Rules, and he approved of the fact that in French drama, which was changing more fundamentally than he realized, those Rules were "usually well observed."[17] But wherever he found fault with infringement of such Rules in new French drama, he objected, not exactly on principle, but because the playwright concerned was offending in some way against "naturalness" or proportion. Likewise, where he censured modern French style, it was for being too "sententious," or "affected," or "inflated." [18]

In his mature breadth of vision he even saw, despite his unchanging reverence for the old French masters whose superiority he took for granted, that France's modern playwrights could cling too closely to tradition. That ancient Greek subject matter with its pagan gods, myths, and moral values, which was acceptable to ancient Greeks and, vicariously, to seventeenth-century Frenchmen, was no longer plausible, he believed, in modern drama of the Age of Reason. This was the explanation, he considered, of the very indifferent success of Voltaire's Greek-minded *Oreste*. This was the explanation of the "false sublimity" of certain other modern tragedies which strained after old effects. When modern spectators wept at performances of Racine's *Phèdre*, he therefore concluded, they must have been weeping not because the force of the tragic subject had been brought home to them, but because Racine's genius and the actress' skill had carried them away. [19]

Unlike some Spanish Gallicists, Luzán was too forward-looking to try to impose on the Spanish theater he wanted to reform in the French image, the oratorical techniques of Parisian playhouses. Acting by declamation seemed to him to be out of keeping with the spirit of an age of reason. Though he realized that traditionally declamatory affectation, as the non-French observer saw it, was suitable for traditional French purposes, and that extraordinary vocal "energy" was needed for the presentation of abnormal Greek passions. Even his qualification here is judicious, however. The genuinely natural, in the sense of purely conversational, method of presenting high tragedy was not yet visualized in all its potentialities. The subtle insinuations of ordinary talk even nowadays are still appreciated by a minority of spectators. Much less exacting were, and are, emotional rant and gesture. "Is this a dagger which I see before me?" still more easily inspires horror if Macbeth frenziedly shouts the line than if it is quietly insinuated; just as the splendid choruses of Handel's *Messiah* increase in value for the average hearer as the sound increases in volume.

But Luzán knew of more natural French actors like Baron, and actresses like Lecouvreur. These had been influenced, a fact he appeared not to know, by the English art of the theater made famous by Garrick and described by A. François Riccoboni, an admirer of English techniques, in his treatise on Dramatic Art.[20] To such an extent had the idea of verisimilitude in acting impressed Luzán, that he translated a portion of Riccoboni's rules for stage movement and gesture.[21] Also, as we learn from Don Juan, he had the intention of following Riccoboni's practical example and writing an Art of the Theater for the Spanish Stage, called, intimidatingly enough, *Treatise on the Perfect Actor*.[22] This might well have been the most self-revealing of all his output. His interpretation of how to react emotionally to given situations would inevitably have exposed, if not his personal experience, at least his personal assessment of the extent to which feelings fluctuate and can naturally be exteriorized. It would expose his judgment of other people's behavior and motives for behavior, and reveal his psychological penetration or his lack of understanding. Of course, a book on histrionic art written by other than an actor-producer could not have ensured stage-naturalness. Even instructions translated from Riccoboni are the more stylized ones concerning posture: rounding the hands instead of clenching them; bending arms from the shoulder instead of from the elbow, and so on. Spanish actors who, however illiterate, had always excelled in comedy by mimicking natural tones, undertones, and overtones, natural action and activity, to the life, would have to adapt a new national rather than a new foreign technique for new serious drama. In any case, eighteenth-century "natural" acting was not what we should understand by "natural" at all. It was not realistic interpretation of the behavior of men under ordinary human strain. It was an interpretation of how the producer and his advisers thought that ideally men ought to want to behave. The two realities, actual and reconstructed, seldom coincided in stage life. Yet Luzán was moving rapidly with his times towards the acceptance of the idea that the Age of Reason, for its drama of reason, needed histrionic reasonableness, needed educated players to represent the exquisite unobviousness of ordinary conversation, needed a professional status for actors of which they need no longer be socially ashamed.

Luzán's practical character is further observable in his comments on physical features of French theaters: architecture, seating, policing, and so on. This was a matter of money, perhaps of the state grants, recently advocated in Spain by those who deplored the slatternly disarray and noisy disorder of Madrid theaters. Observing the efficiency of lighting arrangements, he takes the trouble to count, with solemn precision, the candelabra. Fourteen there were, he says, clearly impressed by such brilliance, each with twelve candles and all this in addition to three dozen candles on the stage itself. The appropriateness, richness, and cleanliness of the costumes he found remarkable too, as, for the times, it must indeed have been. By implication, therefore, the costumes worn in Spanish theaters, and provided by their underpaid wearers, must have struck him as soiled and squalid. The magnificent fixed scene used for French tragedy also roused Luzán's enthusiasm, partly because of the very magnificence of the furnishings, of the great staircase soaring up from the flatness of the stage to suggest splendors out of sight, of wide perspectives through painted stage windows of an entire neighborhood . . . , partly of its very fixedness. For, to this Spaniard's mind, a fixed scene was more conducive to verisimilitude than were changing scenes: a conclusion with which posterity, and non-Classical circles in his own time, have not concurred. Through artistic quarters, then, Luzán moved with relative animation. In his decorous way he unbended. "I don't know," he says with apologetic surprise at himself, as he begins his next chapter on an entirely different topic, "I don't know what the powerful attraction is that has kept me talking about dramatic Poetry for so much longer than I ought. I must now move on to other subjects." [23]

IV *Alarms in Philosophy*

Given Don Ignacio's training in philosophy and his knowledge of philosophical controversies, it is natural that his attention should light on the fact that French philosophers, even within Jesuit colleges, were deserting from the authorities which in Spain were still considered sacrosanct. From the general context of his Chapter XII, "On Philosophy," Don Ignacio's overall impression must be interpreted as vague alarm: "Aristotle and his philosophy are held in total contempt; nobody mentions the Aristotelian system except to laugh at it." Plato is also forgotten, he persists, discomfortedly. Everybody follows a system of his own, or one made up compositely from several different systems.[24]

That he is alarmed, some of his incidental reasoning can prove.

For instance, he objects that the philosophers who now turn for
authority to modern physicists, Newton especially, are not relating
their findings to any soundly proved system of principles, and,
having abandoned the old Logic—that is, the Logic of theoretic
universals and the theoretic organization of evidence by formulae
—are reasoning in the air. Don Ignacio, who had only glimpsed
the vast, independent reaches of scientific unpreconceivedness,
was baffled by the absence of formalities. Modern French authors,
he discovers, argue by irregular techniques and in nonformal
terms. They rely on their own resources. They seize lightly on any
new idea, and, when this is only half understood, they present
it in print. They despise Aristotle, he goes on, carried away by
disapproval, without having read his works. All of them study
Physics, but few, if any, manage to acquire a good Logic or good
Metaphysics. Some follow Descartes, "despite his defects." Most
mathematicians follow Newton, whether because they believe
him to be—Luzán's accent seems to fall naturally on the word
believe—the best authority or simply because he is fashionable.[25]
Even religion—and here the critic's alarm becomes more positive
—even religion is not free from the dangers attendant on illogical
and unmetaphysical ways of thought; "any opinion that glitters a
little finds patrons and applause, and nobody is capable of showing exactly where error lies." [26]

Seldom did Don Ignacio express himself in such emphatic
disparagement. Naturally he himself was bewildered. The average
scholar, trained in the tenets in which he had been trained, did
not expect to have to assess ideas divorced from dogma. If it were
discovered that animal life derived from eggs, that light behaved
in a way not suspected before, his instinct was to search in the
old systems or in modern systems formally proved superior to the
old, for principles or implications into which new evidence could
be fitted, and only then to admit that what experiments had
shown could be scientifically acceptable. Even if in theory this
average scholar could bring himself to believe that, for example,
the ancient Greek interpretation of the universe might not be
completely correct for all time, might not be fundamentally unchanging, as Catholic dogma was assumed to be unchanging, he
could not, in practice, countenance exceptions to universal philosophy without grave mistrust, or at best, inner reservations. When
the advanced scientists and mathematicians took the unparalleled

evidence of individual instruments—the microscope or air pump
—to mean that new scientific discoveries could no longer be interpreted by previous theories of the universe, that in fact all
theory was liable to fall, then the Luzáns of every country were
understandably disturbed. Their problem was not so much that
they were incapable of believing the truth of anything falling
outside Aristotle's omniscient jurisdiction, as that they could not
accept modern ideas dissociated from a coherently modern system
of Metaphysics. If the old system had to go, a fully-developed, all-
comprehensive new system was expected to take its place. Philosophical rest could not be found in fragmentary possibilities. And
Luzán, in his bewilderment, was comforted by a recent treatise
on Philosophy by Maupertuis which, with soothing reconciliation,
presented Metaphysics as the mother of the sciences.[27]

Bewildered though the Luzáns were, however, they were not
apparently dismayed. They might dislike and distrust the new
conception of suspending judgments on isolated findings, and feel
unable to leave the ultimate interpretation and coordination to
scholars yet unborn. But they were not rabid Scholastics, and
they prepared themselves cautiously, honestly, as far as they were
technically able, to assess the modern trend of experimental science. It was at this point in his own preparation that Luzán, while
in Paris, took a five weeks' private course on Experimental Physics
and, in company with two other Spaniards, "four or five" Frenchmen, some Germans, and a number of Englishmen,[28] tried to
acquaint himself with mechanical apparatus and instruments.
This international class, drawing presumably on the still universal
language of academic Latin, studied for three days a week under
the Abbé Nollet of the Academy of Sciences in rooms of the
Gallery of the Louvre, lent, Luzán approvingly noted, by per-
mission of the King.

The Abbé Nollet's method, which Luzán, in his own words,
could not praise too highly, is described as being partly explanatory and partly practical. Luzán's definition is a little vague. After
all, he was used to defining in general terms. It was, he says, an
explanation of the mathematical and physical principles necessary for understanding the nature of the question under review,
the solution of the problem, and the aim of the experiment.[29] All
too evidently this valiant Arts scholar, used to thinking of science
as a form of philosophy, could not follow the whole of his

teacher's explanation. Significantly, he gives no account of the experiments themselves in the technical details of which Father Feijoo would have reveled. Reading between the lines, we are left with the impression that his understanding of the course was of its general aims rather than of its details. Be that as it may, he certainly admits that to derive benefit from such teaching, the student must already be well grounded in Mathematics; further, that to assimilate the whole of the instruction properly, he would need to prepare each lesson carefully from the printed textbook and read it carefully over again after hearing the explanation and seeing the experiments.

Evidently, then, Don Ignacio found the course technically diffi-cult, though he was convinced of the value of the Abbé's method. A far better method, he thought it, than that of teaching Physics by theory alone in university schools where students "argue uselessly on false or shifting principles meaning nothing and satisfying nobody," [30] and where Physics, dissociated from Mathematics, "is a form of utterly hollow verbosity, a useless and sterile occupation." [31]

It is true that Don Ignacio, observing the Abbé's experiments, buttressed though these were by mathematical evidence, saw them in a void of inconclusive rationalism. It is true that he hankered in consequence after some "universal" system into which the results of individual experiments could be fitted, and he did not understand, with the more advanced, that that was impossi-ble, that, perhaps, no fixed, new, universal system would ever again be established for the purpose of relating every particular to an unchanging code of universal values. He had not quite grasped the fact that the Ages of Universals were over. Accord-ingly, despite the evidence his common sense accepted, he feared that experiments might be subject to some "mistakes and errors," especially when "general conclusions were to be drawn from them and new systems based on them," [32] and he considered that they should be related to a good Logic and sound Metaphysics—for instance of Aristotle. Even so, Luzán, the inveterate systematist, had not hidden his head in Aristotelian assumptions, had not con-demned what he did not fully understand. Nor had he avoided scientific subjects altogether when he had every excuse for doing so. He tried to be fair in his observations. His attitude therefore attracts the respectful attention of posterity at least. It shows that in the loud, scientific and philosophical conflicts of the eighteenth century, there were in Spain, as elsewhere, moderate men willing to consider the reasons of unfamiliar subjects.

Discussion of philosophical institutions and techniques brings him inevitably to that sacred and sublime area of Metaphysics, Theology: slippery ground which he makes no attempt to by-pass. His views, explicit and implied, on the subject are made abundantly clear in chapters like "On Theology and Sacred Oratory" (Chapter XVIII), and "On the Sorbonne" (Chapter XX), the last referring to an institution still theological. It was impossible, in the mental circumstances in which Luzán found himself, to ignore the question as to whether the Scholastic system should be defended or not. The fact that he does not himself step into the arena, as Feijoo did, is beside the point. His interested position among the onlookers is as important in its way as Feijoo's commitment. First he remarks that Scholastic Theology is taught at the Sorbonne and the University College with "notable acumen," that also it is taught by religious, in their own Houses where the Scholastic textbooks of the Dominicans are the works of St. Thomas Aquinas and of Scotus, and those of the Jesuits are the works of the Jesuit Scholastic Suárez.[33] As on previous occasions, Luzán's own views may be gauged from his unextended comments. One of the learned Jesuits of the Paris House, he states with obvious approval of their judgment, told him that there they adhered to Father Suárez' teaching "only so far as they thought it good and reasonable." [34] The statement is left insinuatingly to find its own level of liberal reason.

In other words, Luzán regarded the Paris Jesuits as moderns in moderation, men like himself. He was not, by training or reason, ready to countenance a complete overthrow of the Scholastic systematization of Theology. A technique of relating the particular to the general and universal inspired confidence and taught coherence. But Luzán was too practical to overlook the unpractical element in Scholasticism, to put all his faith in its untested assumptions and wastefully dialectic techniques. Evidently what reasonable Jesuits of the eighteenth century wanted was a revised, modernized Suárez permitting the integration of Scholasticism with newer philosophies. This Luzán could well have understood. His own technique was eclectic. The trouble was, and always has been however, that it is easier to destroy a system completely than to reform it constructively by integration. And Luzán was not destructive. Accordingly his very restraint on this major, impassioned subject is, in the circumstances, more eloquent than a chapterful of explanation. It registers the critical watchfulness of a man not easily swayed by one side of a question exclusively.

Luzán was also pleased with the straightforward sermons he heard in Paris. Never did he hear one there, he said emphatically, that did not leave him well instructed, edified, and contrite. In fact, his approval of Paris preachers roused him to one of his most vehement passages. It brought him, by comparison, to the standard of preaching in Spain, and, specialist in words that he was, strengthened his realization of Spanish disorder. All that "puerile affectation of clauses," the "rhythmical parallelisms of wordplay," the "decadent, booming rhetoric," the "false conceits," the "poetic imagery," and the "popular verses"; all the "juxtaposing of Claudian and Virgil, St. Paul and the Evangelists"; the "nonsensical misapplication of texts"; the "execrable allusions . . . which are an insult to religion and are received with horror by the well instructed of the Faithful . . ." [35]—all that misuse of language and meaning, confirmed by other responsible critics of Spain's pulpit affairs, was a subject capable of rousing him much more naturally to excitement than were the half-comprehensible experiments in world-shaking realities of the Abbé Nollet.

Heartfelt though this outburst is, within the quiet context of Luzán's reflections, it is not nearly so self-revealing as the sustained indictment of his final chapter, "On Some Modern Books and Authors," though, again, it is in the literary approach to contemporary realities that he is most outspoken. Courteously placed at the end of what has been, for the most part, an admiring study of French ideas and techniques, come the French defects. Had Luzán been nothing more than a starry-eyed admirer of the French way of life, we should have discredited his general testimony. But he does not provoke our cynicism. Intelligent travelers, he knew, must observe "the good and the bad . . ." of foreign regions, herbs of medicinal values, and "herbs that are noxious." [36] In the Paris publishing world, goes his deliberately constructed introduction to the chapter, there are, despite innumerable works of value—he specially mentions Montesquieu's De l'Esprit des Lois which greatly influenced Spain's reform of Economics—other books "which for the poison they contain or the scandal they cause or consequences they entail, may be considered the poisonous and deadly productions of this pleasant and most fertile country." [37]

At this point Luzán's modern readers, supposing that such a torrent of disapproval from so mild a man must be leading up to an attack on those anti-Catholic extremists, the Deists, are somewhat disconcerted by his primary example of corruption: the popular novels just then pouring from the press in splashes of publicity. He was fair enough to admit the stylistic grace and naturalness of most of them. But what he could not approve was "license and even indecency" in the manners they depicted, and he feared that their influence "little by little would make the nation effeminate, and destroy its taste for more profitable works." [38] When we reflect, however, on the nature of certain of these novels to which he so strongly objected—for example on *"Theresa the Philosopher,"* by which, presumably, he means P. Bridard de la Garde's *Lettres de Thérèse* . . . ,[39] Luzán appears less obscurantist than his attack might at first suggest. This novel, bearing significant likenesses to parts of Richardson's *Pamela,* has for its heroine a philosophizing, female letter-writer, who, if not engaging directly in dubious love affairs, deals with them vicariously and, like the Pamela of the later part of Richardson's story, indulges in advice and criticism on all manner of subjects with the popular sentimentality of the lower order of artists.

Still, as if to defend himself against a charge of intellectual prejudice, Luzán goes on reasonably to explain that a novel should not be censured simply because it is a novel. Even, astonishingly, he regrets the passing of the old Novels of Chivalry, that is, the Arthurian tales and their Spanish equivalents—killed, he rather inaccurately assumes, by Cervantes' laughter in *Don Quijote*. At least the chivalresque inspires valor, good faith, and honor unto death, run his thoughts, whereas the new French novels inspire nothing but love, pleasure, and lasciviousness, and are all the more harmful in an age when Europe as a whole is growing demoralized by ease and idleness.

Here, then, is the real reason for Luzán's disgust. Spaniards, the Aragonese conspicuously among them, revered, and still revere, the ideal of manliness, which is why Don Juan in his excesses represents an extreme acceptable to Spanish understanding;

why sword-play and the arrogant point-of-honor have figured so largely in Spanish literature. The opposite extreme of effeminacy is distasteful to Peninsular mentality. Besides, the Inquisition disapproved of languorous love-making in print and on the stage, believing, like the English guardians of public morals who in earlier times had caused girls' parts to be played on the stage by boys, that men's passions are titillated by visual representations of amorousness and that these put frivolous ideas into giddy young heads. Luzán's argument, then, was not due to the fact that he was too easily shocked. It meant that he looked for better ideals of behavior than popular novels provided, and realized, as do many people who nowadays fear the influence of television, that the average reader who, instead of judging a book, identifies himself with it, can be powerfully influenced by what he uncritically absorbs.

Eventually, as anticipated, Don Ignacio does come to the Deists exemplified for purposes of the *Memoirs* by a singularly harmful book, he says, entitled *Les Moeurs (Customs)* and dealing with Deist philosophy. This will be Voltaire's anonymously published *Essai sur l'Histoire Générale et sur les Moeurs et l'Esprit des Nations* . . . which was burnt, Luzán explains, by the public hangman but which is not yet dead.[40] Indeed, what he so greatly deplores is the fact that it has been widely translated and republished clandestinely; worst of all, that its pleasing style and lively descriptions have already made it widely acceptable. He would be thinking especially no doubt of Voltaire's rationalistic attitude in a history of peoples which disregarded their religious excuses for warlike behavior and belittled their reliance on Providence.

Nevertheless, Luzán had the curiosity to meet and take the opportunity of speaking to the author of this history, albeit, one may assume, in some public gathering where he could hardly have avoided him. He carefully refrains from naming him in this context, saying, with a certain pleasing irony not overcommon in his solemn works, that probably the author will come to be glad of the fact that Luzán has not revealed his name, particularly in view of the possibility that one day he may realize the error of his ways.

When all is explained, then, we find our respect for Luzán increasing during the course of his *Paris Memoirs*. As a mature scholar, he was not easily influenced by what he saw and heard.

Neither, however, did he primly or prudishly shut his mind to the worst of what was going on around him. Rather he attempted to judge, certainly by inherited standards, yet to judge fairly. He passes through his *Memoirs* like an honest scholar, typical of the honest, middle-way scholars of any century, whose role is not to lead but assess leadership, whose greatest asset is his sense of proportion, who may not be able to foretell the likely future, but who can analyze immediate alarms: in short, he provides us with a means of calculating how much, at best, the leader-visionaries of any given period can hope to be understood by their own contemporaries.

CHAPTER 4

Experiment in Drama

LUZÁN'S dramatic potentialities must be gauged largely from his insight as a translator. But we believe those potentialities to have been genuinely realizable and to have been tuned to the analytical mood of his epoch. One practical result of his stay in Paris was a change of direction in his dramatic thinking. From our knowledge of his work before 1750, of the first edition of the *Poetics,* of his lyrics, of his interests in music and art, we should expect him to translate some splendid model tragedy, or some heroic drama of Classical proportions and Italian warmth of imagery. There is nothing surprising, therefore, about his choice, in 1747, of the Italian librettist, Metastasio, whose dramas are as Classically decorous as they are verbally imaginative.[1] Luzán was poet enough to be able to enter into the Metastasian spirit, though not poet enough to propagate Metastasio's spirit with any originality. Diverted, however, as the *Paris Memoirs* reveals, along novel French ways of reasoning, Luzán came to a less obviously heroic region than that of grand Italian opera, and discovered a new source of interest in the dramatic impact of the common problems of commoners in common circumstances, and of the vast possibilities for drama of ordinary human thought-processes. Thus again, we are not surprised when, sometime between 1750 and 1751, he translated a modern, middle-class problem or thesis play from the French of the advanced playwright Nivelle de la Chaussée, as a preliminary, perhaps, if only his health could have permitted it, to writing an original drama in the same style. At last he appeared to have found his creative bent. So absorbed by now was he in La Chaussée's psychological insinuations, and so sensitively did he interpret them, that his potentialities for dramatic creativeness in the medium of the realistic and commonplace speak through his translation for themselves.

I   *La virtud coronada (Virtue Crowned)*

What does surprise posterity about this strict Preceptist, is that Luzán's earliest dramatic experiment, in 1742 or thereabouts, was a sensation-crowded, heroic drama which broke most of the Rules of Art that he had solemnly propounded in the *Poetics* a few years before.

Between 1737, when his *Poetics* was published, and 1747, when he entered upon his diplomatic career, Luzán seems to have spent much of his time quietly writing at the family estate of Monzón in Aragon. There he worked on historical and political treatises.[2] But he was also occupied at the time, his son tells us, in translating certain works from the Italian.[3] When, therefore, about 1742, he wrote a drama for private performance at the local Town Hall in Monzón, with various ladies and gentlemen of the vicinity taking part as actors, we are not unprepared for the Italian atmosphere of this play. It is entitled *La virtud coronada (Virtue Crowned)* and appeared to disconcert Luzán's son who felt himself obliged to suggest that its irregularities would doubtless be due to Don Ignacio's tolerant condescension to the wishes of his Monzón friends. For *Virtue Crowned,* the biographer-son had to admit, did not "observe the Rules of Art with that exactitude which would be expected from one who had taught and defended them so intelligently and consistently." [4]

Virtue Crowned has, in fact, every appearance of being another translation, adaptation, or recast from the Italian, though Don Juan does not seem to suspect this, and we have been unable to trace an Italian original. The play is extant in manuscript in the Royal Academy of History in Madrid, and, while bearing no name of author, it corresponds to Don Juan's description and figures among Luzán's papers held by the Academy.

Certainly, in some obvious ways, this serious drama is curiously unclassical, yet in others is as curiously Luzanesque. Among its unclassical features, probably the most remarkable is the comic character, Bretón, who is so unnecessary to the complicated intrigue that he not only helps to destroy a Classical Unity of Action, but looks as if he had been inserted after the play was written, as perhaps he had. In rehearsal, either in Monzón or elsewhere, the drama may have proved too solemn for a mixed group of amateur actors and for a fiesta-audience expecting excitement to be laced with gaiety. Unclassical, too, for instance, are the frequent changes of scene within the acts, though, for reasons to be discussed a little later, this phenomenon is less strange than the mixture of comedy and seriousness. On the other hand, Luzán's mind or approval is very evident in the elaborate, moral seriousness of the drama as a whole, in the importance given to ordinary, intelligent reasoning, even where that reasoning is clumsily inexpert, in the mentality of the philosopher Philodemo with whom Luzán seems privately to be identifying himself, and in the rational if somewhat bookish principles of the high-minded hero, Cyro. By his moral theme and by the rational conversation of the play, Luzán might have been trying to provide a model of the profoundly serious, responsible drama he wanted Spain to adopt.

The complicated *Virtue Crowned,* written in varied meters and in three acts, tells of an uneasy state of alliance between the ancient Medes and Persians; of military aid brought by the Persian Prince Cyro (Cyrus) to his uncle Astyages, usurper King of the Medes, who is governing for his niece by marriage, the uncomplaining Fenisa; of Astyages' fear and jealousy of Cyro who is capturing all hearts and whom the populace is liable to see as a suitable husband for Fenisa and set him up in Astyages' place; of attempts to distract Cyro's attention and undermine his energy by encouraging him to fall in love with a beautiful Persian prisoner, Berenice; of the double-dealing of the double-dyed villain, Asebandro, whose secret intention is to kill Astyages, Cyro, and probably Fenisa too, marry Berenice and establish himself as king; of Cyro's happy and Asebandro's fatal issue from plots and counterplots, and from a highly inverisimilar climax studded with poison cups and unpoisoned cups confusingly substituted for each other by both accident and design; and of Cyro's forgiving reconciliation with Astyages, who eventually names the Persian Prince as his successor and Fenisa as Cyro's bride.

Indirectly involved in this plot of sophisticated ambiguities, coincidences, disguised intentions, mistaken identities, and even, at times, sword play, is the Philosopher, Philodemo, who holds the balance for good against the machinations of Asebandro and who, by being on the right stage-spot at the right time, saves the life of Cyro. Another indirect agent of justice is the comic Bretón, whose chief business is to crack timid jokes, but whose bustling officiousness causes him to succor the wounded Asebandro with what he, Bretón, takes to be a cup of water, and which is really a cup of poison intended by Asebandro for Cyro. The spectacular characters are "as many soldiers as may seem suitable," [5] who stride in to the accompaniment of martial music, and the scene-filling retinues of King, Princes, and other important persons.

In fact, if Nasarre could argue that the plays of Cervantes were parodies of the plays of Lope de Vega, with how much more justification might it be argued that *Virtue Crowned* was a parody of the heroic libretti of Metastasio. Nevertheless internal evidence proves that *Virtue Crowned* was meant to be serious heroic drama. The play righteously presents, to quote the converted Astyages at the end of his exhaustingly crooked career, "the most heroic and rarest example of moderation ever witnessed." [6] And all the earnest strength of Luzán's message is contained in that thougtful word "moderation" which represents an ideal, un-dramatic, perhaps, in the context of Spanish dramatic tradition, but forceful enough in the new eighteenth-century context of bourgeois thesis drama, an example of which Luzán was soon to translate. Undeniably the serious lesson of *Virtue Crowned* is too explicit, though frequently the process of moral reasoning is worthy of a much better drama, or of more expert distribution. In the end all characters are restored to their right minds by their reason whcih is deliberately brought to bear on the compelling force of their experience. Asebandro is the one exception. Yet even he at the point of death harangues the audience about his own iniquity and formally recognizes the justice of his punish-ment.

Although *Virtue Crowned* was intended as a heroic drama, the heroic element—if Bretón is excluded—was in the stately Italian tradition of opera, as exemplified in, let us say, Metastasio's *At-tilio Regolo*. Its worst artistic feature we should now describe as its "melodrama"—a word originally used of the combination of drama and music and later associated with the pretentious, ex-aggerated posturing of figures in opera where realism is sub-ordinated to music. Most Spanish writers of Neoclassical tragedy in the eighteenth century were more melodramatic than tragic, and many scenes in Nicolás Fernández de Moratín's *Hormesinda*, for instance, now seem quite as unintentionally comic as do Luzán's. The lesson which Don Ignacio ought to have learnt from his experiment was that he could not express himself convincingly in large-scale heroics.

Outstanding Metastasian features of the drama are the stage directions for imposing scenery which, with the backing of the Aragonese nobility of Luzán's home-province, was doubtless acquired, in most of its detail, for the Town Hall in Monzón. There are directions for a panorama of a wide countryside with the town of the Medes on the one hand, and with hills on the other—presumably three-dimensional hills since "as many soldiers as may seem convenient" are instructed to file down to the stage from between the slopes, to the accompaniment of a solemn military march. There are indoor sets for King Astyages' palace. There are trees beneath which characters sing and play instruments, and formal gardens described somewhat disdainfully by Cyro as "daughters of artifice." [7] for Cyro, like the Aragonese who just then was Luzán, preferred, he said, "the natural beauty of the hills." And there is a dungeon where Cyro languishes in chains, and which is so dark that all manner of intriguers, with or without poison cups, surreptitiously flit in and out at will. Surely all this could not be represented on one backcloth only, however ingeniously contrived. We wonder, therefore, if Luzán, who in the *Poetics* of 1737 had spoken with great enthusiasm of Dr. Baruffaldi's theory of simultaneous settings—horizontal or vertical—to permit variety of scene while preserving the Unity of Place, might not have experimented in some such way at the Town Hall of Monzón. If so, he probably found practice less verisimilar than theory. Which may account for his much decreased enthusiasm over the Baruffaldi project in the second edition of his *Poetics*.[8]

But by far the most determined and earnestly sustained feature of *Virtue Crowned* is its projection of moral responsibility. Not only is the entire drama resolutely directed towards the triumph of justice and integrity; not only does Cyro, the heroic model of moderation whose virtue is crowned with success, have a right judgment in all things and at every possible moment, suitable and unsuitable, philosophize on personal and public obligations, to the point of sententiousness, but all the people of the play, at some time or other, deliver themselves self-consciously of thoughtful remarks. The very villains, once they have repented or come to well-merited grief, chime in the chorus of analytical didacticism. Some of this philosophizing, too, is genuinely and intrinsically impressive and would have been far more noticeable if it had been less prolific. Much of it echoes what must have been Luzán's own sentiments about the unspectacular virtues on which he would be likely to pride himself: integrity, perhaps in face of easy publicity; wisdom as opposed to opinionatedness. Cyro, early in Act I, goes out of his way to desire in words that no star save virtue may guide his valor; in Act II he varies the sentiment by observing that any one virtue has different effects on different temperaments—an interesting suggestion that might have been developed enthrallingly by a better playwright. In prison, in Act III, Cyro is inclined to preach more rantingly and consequently becomes less effective. What he believes to be his last utterance on earth is mouthed with such stagy pathos that one is reminded of many dying heroes in the Spanish parodies of Neoclassical tragedy, that were so much more successful than the original tragedies they burlesqued.[9]

Despite its shaky, occasionally ludicrous technique, however, *Virtue Crowned* represents an enterprising desire to assert the importance of thoughtful reasonableness in drama, not just as a general moral message pronounced at crises by the hero, but as an intricate pattern of mental behavior throughout every major and minor scene. The cynicism of malicious characters, for instance, is often rationalized acceptably. Obstacles, says the cynical King, not without truth, "are broken down by power, and interest facilitates the riskiest of ventures."[10] "Politics," adds Asebandro, realistically, "requires skill rather than force."[11] Their remarks, therefore, indicate experience and a certain brand of practical philosophy that makes conflict reasonable. In general, too, these intriguers think over all possibilities before making their decisions, by a basic rule of common sense which had not been much in evidence in Spanish heroic drama, but which was essential to the development of rational heroics in the eighteenth century. Even the subject of love provokes a semi-intellectual discussion between Fenisa and Cyro about higher and lower forms of the love-passion. Cyro, speaking on behalf of higher ideals, rises to a religious level by suggesting to Fenisa that her assumption of many gods is false. While she, academically, doubts if love and virtue can reside together in the same person. The whole argument is cast in the intellectual tone of La Chaussée's

Le Préjugé à la mode (Man of Modish Taboos) which Luzán, evidently fascinated by the complex possibilities of mental relationships, was soon to translate. Perhaps Don Ignacio was specially interested in the mental problems produced by love and marriage because by now he himself had married. It would be typical of him to try to analyze and ethically judge any emotional experience.

There is also, in dramatic parenthesis, a deliberately engineered problem of friendship worked out between Cyro and Cloriarco, Prince of Egypt, his ally. Both have opportunities for expressing the noble misunderstandings and noble reconciliations, with noble speeches to match, which the century acquired from Voltaire, who acquired them from Addison, who acquired them from Shakespeare.

Most meaningful of all the characters, however, is the philosopher Philodemo who stands usually just outside the plot. Some of his pronouncements are conventionally didactic and unimpressive. We can only sympathize with Bretón—behind Luzán's back —when he says that "the old man is tedious." [12] But other remarks of Philodemo seem to be edged with the eighteenth-century interest of Luzán, or of his source, or of both. In Act I, Philodemo deplores the present state of affairs in the capital city of the Medes and sighs as he thinks of less decadent times, when every man seemed to be appropriately employed, when the nobles exercised moderation, when their sons were properly brought up, when respect was paid to elders, when sincerity prevailed. Nowadays, finds Philodemo, projecting his ulterior motives over Italian and Spanish courts and capitals of the eighteenth century, court society is corrupt with double-dealing, flattery, and luxury. Wherefore he seriously advises Cyro not to trust anyone at court but merely to be agreeable to all. "Let fools," he tells him, "think that to be humane is to be weak, and that docility is a form of ignorance. The wise man understands, penetrates, recognizes the astute sham of political talents without ever imitating them." [13] This sounds like the experience of the quiet Luzán whose modesty and unobtrusiveness in high circles, which he would know intimately, must often have been taken for ignorance or inadequacy. Indeed it would not be unnatural if, in his dependent circumstances, he had developed some sense of inferiority and had learned to rely on his academic attainments alone as the rock-source of personal self-confidence. Certainly there is some slight suggestion of self-righteousness in Philodemo similar to the self-righteousness of the Golden Age hunchback playwright Ruiz de Alarcón, whose inferiority complex took refuge in his drama. The weighted proverb used as a title for Alarcón's *Las paredes oyen (Walls have Ears)* is quoted by Luzán-Philodemo in Act I, though probably by sheer coincidence. Further, it is noteworthy that Cyro's idealism is ascribed by King Astyages and Asebandro to too much theorizing and book-learning (Act II), accusations which are made against most academic men and which Luzán must surely have heard often about himself from his lay friends and relations. In any case, whether Philodemo is speaking for Luzán, or whether Luzán is identifying himself with the Philodemo of some source-play, direct or vicarious experience is being drawn upon and is dramatically effective. So long as the playwright left all of his own experience entirely outside his drama, that drama would be unlifelike, stiff, and, said eighteenth-century Spanish critics of Neoclassical drama, "cold." Here was a demonstration of how one kind of life could be infused into stage-statues.

Altogether, then, *Virtue Crowned,* if artistically inexpert, is a respectable attempt to present serious, lifelike reasoning and characterization, and is a better model, by far, than the "cold" rhetorical models of Nicolás Fernández de Moratín who figures much more conspicuously in dramatic history. Too much is attempted in *Virtue Crowned.* There is too much intriguing, too much didacticism, too much melodrama. But the play offers usefully debatable ideas and demonstrates the practical technique of reasoning aloud in stage conversation. Finally, but not of least importance, Luzán's verse, with its graceful Classical similes and effective sobriety of image, shows how some poet, more original than he, might attain with sober reason to the "wonders" and "marvels" that Luzán instinctively connected with elevated style and diction.

II *The Allure of Opera*

By 1747, several works of Metastasio, the most successful librettist of Luzán's times, were well known in Spain, had found favor with the Spanish Bourbon King Felipe V and his Italian queen, and had been elaborately staged for royal performances under the direction of Metastasio's friend, the Italian singer

Farinelli, whose services were engaged by the Spanish court in 1737. Performances were given sometimes in Italian, sometimes in Spanish. But it should be remembered, first, that Italian, being a language akin to Spanish, would not be wholly incomprehensible to a Spanish audience; secondly, that, since Italian syllables and word forms are roughly similar to Spanish, they lend themselves easily to literal verse translation. Later Bourbon kings of Spain preserved the musical connection with Italy.

Most readily must Luzán have accepted a commission to translate Metastasio's *La Clemenza di Tito (The Clemency of Titus)* [14] for a royal command performance in 1747. The drama of the world-famous Metastasio was culturally distinguished, high-minded, Classical in theme and construction, noble in sentiment and expression. And who more obvious than the Italian-educated, Italian-speaking, Italian-orientated Spanish gentleman-poet to translate Metastasio's glow and ardor into Spanish incandescence for an aristocratic Spanish audience? Luzán, too, understood music, and could handle the libretto with greater sensibility for that reason. Further, Metastasio was a poet who could commend to Spanish audiences the Classical tastes which Don Ignacio had been advocating in his *Poetics*. As a librettist Metastasio, by tacit Preceptist consent, was able to take more liberties with Aristotelian Rules of Art than the straight dramatist and seemed to Spain more vivacious than French Classicists. Rendered airborne by his alliance with music, he could demonstrate his right to soar above the head of reason, especially in emotional scenes, and to indulge in the licensed lyrics and insinuating rhythms which intensify his love scenes, and turn the starkness of tragedy into radiance. By dint of genius, by the authority of Preceptists, Metastasio was capable of making tragedy emotionally attractive.

Luzán, a literary purist, would not easily deceive himself. But at least a minor reason for the obvious interest with which he translated Metastasio would be that the works of this Italian, which appealed to his musical ear, also appealed to his painter's eye. Certainly, when he translated the work for performance before the recently crowned Fernando VI in the Carnival season of 1747, he reduced none of Metastasio's stage directions.

Nor did he fail to set Metastasio's intrigue—a conspiracy to overthrow the Emperor Titus in which the Emperor's friend,

Sextus, had become distressedly involved—on that linguistic level of dignified reasonableness where Metastasio, dramatically speaking, was at his best. If the characters in Spanish exclaim too much, exposing inner fears which should have been subtly insinuated, they exclaim out of Metastasian necessity.

The high quality of Luzán's translation becomes conspicuous when this is compared with an earlier, unimaginative, word-for-word translation into Spanish of the same work by P. F. Quazza.[15] Significantly, Quazza who, like Luzán, was under the obligation to cut the drama to the measurement of Spanish stage performance, made different abridgments from those judiciously made by his successor. Don Ignacio cuts certain aria lines, attractive but unnecessary. Quazza cuts the impressively philosophical remarks on justice pronounced by Titus.[16] Luzán, presumably for diplomatic reasons of seemliness of occasion and good taste, cuts lines in which Metastasio moralizes tediously on the duties of princes, where he states all too obviously that the monarch should distrust flatterers near the throne, and that ruling would be a pleasure if every person close to the monarch were a person of integrity.[17] Luzán avoids unnecessary declamation and rhetorical emphasis. When characters make decisions with lyrically meditative reasonableness, when Sextus, for example, bravely prepares for death, reminding himself of his original intention to betray his sovereign and of the predicament to which his sin of intention has logically led him, Luzán selects imaginatively rhythmical equivalents of natural Spanish thoughtfulness and pathos. Quazza, at the first suggestion of emotion, breaks into rhetorical invocation. For the straightforward Italian "Now do I go to death in very truth and with my courage high . . ."— translated by Luzán as "And now I know that I am going to death, and, with my courage high *(arrestrado)*, I fear it not . . ."— he supplies the insensate, because implausible, vocative "Oh. cruel fate! Yet haughtily *(airado)* I look upon my death." [18]

Not that a singer would be placed at a disadvantage by Quazza's attitudinizing. But Luzán's *Clemency of Titus* is the better contribution to literature.

III   *The Cult of the Ordinary*

Luzán's interest in La Chaussée's *The Man of Modish Taboos* [19] was due to a more mature awareness of modern trends of thinking. In La Chaussée and his English compeers, George Lillo and Edward Moore, we witness a determined attempt to investigate ordinary domestic problems, not in the old comic sense of exteriorizing by farce the typical defects of types of people and societies, not with the self-righteous idea of distributing exact poetic justice among the conventional representatives of right and wrong, but in the modern sense of analyzing the reason behind illogical sensibilities and mental maladjustments where the difference between right and wrong is relative instead of absolute: the sense in which La Chaussée examines the reason behind one form of marital unhappiness. In this anti-heroic drama we are introduced gradually to the problems of a married couple, D'Urval and Constance, who genuinely love one another. Incidentally we come upon those of Sophie, Constance's cousin, and Damon, the young man to whom Sophie is engaged. One of the best features of the work is Sophie's mistrust of the married state when she reflects on the obviously, yet inexplicably, unhappy marriage of her cousin. Her consequent hesitation in giving her final word to marry someone to whom she is devoted, the distress of Argant, her uncle and Constance's father, and of her fiancé who cannot understand how such fear and mistrust can have been generated, produce rational nervousness of a high dramatic order. Powerfully dominating the entire drama is the tense bafflement of all the characters concerned, and the plot is complicated with certain refinements of self-torture.

Rather less convincing from the Spanish point of view, as Luzán implies in his critical Dedication, was the ultimate reason for the misery of the married pair.[20] On evidence supplied for us by the scientifically minded Memoranda for the History of Science and Letters [21] of Trévoux, certain circles of sophisticated French upper classes, turning with something of the cynicism which nowadays is occasionally directed against devoted married couples by those who despise the sameness of stability and the "middle-class stodginess" of traditional loyalties, were making a fashionable parade of their real or affected indifference to conjugal affection and conjugal values. As a result, says the Memoranda . . . , the younger members of these circles were predisposed to sophisticated disparagement. On such nervous and unnatural tensions of sophistication La Chaussée's play is based.

When translating La Chaussée, Luzán made a few suggestive changes. He gave the characters Spanish names, the better to commend them to Spanish experience. More significantly, he slightly changed the title, with its air of Frenchified artificiality, to the more fundamental *La razón contra la moda (Reason versus Convention)*, because the case brought up by Reason against all Prejudice, whether of fashion past or present, was to Don Ignacio's legal mind a case to be defended instinctively. "Reason," at all events, is the word we most naturally associate with him. He also changed the French couplets, disliked by Spaniards for their monotony, into traditional Spanish *romance*, the ballad line, which moves rapidly for narration, meditation, or exchange of dialogue, and which, with its rhyme of vowels only, adapts itself as easily to dramatic purposes as does English blank verse. Another external point of interest is that his translation is dedicated, under the pseudonym of "The Wanderer," to the Lady President of the Academy of Good Taste where it must have been read and discussed. Which means that the experiment was not completed in mental isolation, but that, directly or indirectly, positively or negatively, it affected an influential group of thinkers. In this respect, in his presentation to the intelligentsia of a modern form of drama in which the emphasis is placed almost entirely on the subtleties of ordinary conversation, Luzán was performing one of his most lasting services to the cultural development of his country. Here was a practical exhibition to Spain's Age of Reason of how modern man reasoned.

Its importance and Luzán's general prestige were duly recognized in a French review of his translation appearing in the *Memoranda for the History of Science and Letters* of January, 1752, which describes his work as one of the first fruits of that "brilliant society, the Marchioness de Sarria's Academy of Good Taste." [22] The reviewer, pleased to find in a Spaniard the somewhat rare penchant for French principles of literature, speaks of Luzán's first-hand knowledge of France and French culture, and applauds his good taste in discriminating between what in France is "good and estimable and what is merely popular and frivolous." [23] Discrimination is a quality which we have already learned to attribute to Luzán. And the *Memoranda* . . . , like Luzán himself, is indirectly censuring various forms of subliterature or semiliterature, particularly popular novelettes, and the commercial propaganda which made them so conspicuous.

Naturally Luzán had commended himself initially to the *Memoranda*'s esteem by the Classical tone of his *Poetics* of 1737. The reviewer comments with paternal approval on Luzán's insistence that the Rules of Art, including the Dramatic Unities, should be strictly observed even in comedy.[24] He also takes the trouble to defend Luzán's use of Spanish meters, explaining to the ignorant that the Spanish *romance* is a genuine verse form and that the translation is not, as some misguided Frenchmen might think, a mixture of verse and prose. So determined is the *Memoranda* to treat Luzán's country fairly, that the author cuts across French prejudice to the extent of commending the Spanish *romance* for its advantages of flexibility and naturalness: a great concession for a French dramatic critic. The *Memoranda* certainly was one of the most open-minded of European reviews. But, even so, we are surprised to hear it rejoice, that "all our caprices, all our attitudes, all our fantasies, all our excesses, all our vices have not yet crossed the frontiers of the Pyrenees," [25] and that the customs depicted in *The Man of Modish Taboos* are not—as yet—typical of Spain. Being, too, a periodical inclining always to scientific analysis, the *Memoranda* now tries to trace French conjugal sophistications to their source, and stops to discuss the history of the particular form of sophisticated silliness correctly taken from French life by La Chaussée. To judge from its tone and emphasis, the *Memoranda* was gratified that Luzán should contribute, with his foreign arms, to the destruction of undesirable French practices. In short, the *Memoranda* thoroughly approved of Luzán and his translation, and, by favoring him, it brought the Aragonese to an international notice which few Frenchmen during the eighteenth century were willing to accord to Spaniards.

Don Ignacio was not the man to accept models, methods, or judgments, least of all from modern authors, with uncritical admiration. In this instance he devotes part of his prefatory discourse to a criticism of La Chaussée's inadequacy. As a reasoned believer in the psychological value of the Unities, Luzán could not be expected entirely to approve of La Chaussée's double action which crossed the problems of one pair of characters with those of another, giving them almost equal importance. But this was so slight an infringement of the Unity of Action, and, moreover, says Luzán, determined not to detract from La Chaussée's prestige, the two sets of action are so well worked together that the audience would not be distracted. For his own part Don Ignacio does not press this criticism.

A much more serious defect mentioned by him is La Chaussée's cheap contrivance of extraneous letters and portraits to complicate the intrigue. For this was a physical means of furthering plot development that had been done to death in all countries, and kept the emphasis on externals. Since such contrivances did not virtually transgress against Classical laws, it is all the more to Luzán's credit that he deplored the dependence of a mental conflict on artificially material means. He seemed to have entered so wholeheartedly into the spirit of the original problem—alien though it was to his Spanish or Italian context—that any deviation from its natural line of tension would diminish for him the force of the play's psychology.

Most remarkable of all are Luzán's diffident comments on dramatic asides and soliloquies which La Chaussée and nearly all playwrights of his period took for granted. When we remember that dramatic asides were used in new works down to the twentieth century, in the Spanish Jacinto Benavente, for example, our respect for the few eighteenth-century Preceptists who called them unrealistic, and the few dramatists—Montiano y Luyando, for instance—who dispensed with them altogether,[26] must surely increase. For this was one of the features of old drama which the new critic, by practical experiment, by observing and analyzing plays as they were being performed, found unacceptably incongruous; just as the new scientists, in the process of experiment, came upon incongruities in ancient theories and studied methods of eliminating them.

But because it took nearly two hundred years to plan dramas in which the characters' private feelings could be made to manifest themselves indirectly, and the audience forced to imagine for itself the words suggested by actors' silences and authors' suppressions, the eighteenth century was still not in a position to prescribe for alternatives to asides and soliloquies. Luzán therefore found himself in a quandary, and, while disliking dramatic artificialities of communication, he had the common sense to acknowledge that the suppression of asides or soliloquies might lead to roundabout explanations more unnatural yet.[27] It is true that on this subject Luzán was rather less knowledgeable than Montiano. But, between them, they publicized the desirability of stage realism and were the earliest Spanish forerunners of the theory of lifelike histrionics.

PART II

Testimony of the *Poetics*

CHAPTER 5

The Poetics. *Problems of the Two Editions, 1737 and 1789*[1]

I *History of the Editions*

A history of the changes introduced into the posthumous, second edition of the *Poetics* is outlined by the publisher Antonio de Sancha, in conjunction with the editor, Luzán's friend and protégé Eugenio de Llaguno y Amírola, in an "Editor's Address to the Readers." Sancha—the publisher writes in the first person and refers to Llaguno in the third—explains that when he was preparing a second edition of the *Poetics*, he was put into touch first with Eugenio de Llaguno who possessed certain notes, made by Luzán himself for a second edition, on a copy of the 1737 original and also on loose pages. Later, Sancha was told that Luzán's son Don Juan also hoped to prepare a second edition, and that the notes had been forwarded to Don Juan for this purpose. After some correspondence, Sancha elaborates, all parties agreed to entrust the publication of a second edition to him, Don Juan returning the separate sheets of manuscript and the manuscript notes on the printed 1737 text in the same state in which he had received them, and furnishing a biography of his father; Llaguno, as editor, then making all necessary corrections, and developing some of Luzán's notes in certain places. Mention is made specifically of rectifications in sections on the history of Spanish versification and dramatic poetry. Incidentally, Sancha remarks that his second edition was meant as an improvement on the 1737 version, which Luzán had had to prepare in Zaragoza with few means at his disposal.

Unfortunately, Luzán's papers containing his alterations to the 1737 text and his notes for a new, augmented edition of it, seem to have disappeared. But in the Gayangos collection of manuscripts of the National Library of Spain, there is a small folder of letters and notes surviving from a correspondence among Don Juan, Antonio de Sancha, and one or two other persons concerned with the 1789 transaction. Several of the papers in the folder refer to the alterations to the 1737 text, saying that Luzán had made them himself. This, from all accounts, was true. The full story of these alterations, however, is rather more complicated than would at first appear. And the most interesting of the Gayangos documents, for our purposes, is an informal memorandum, which proves on internal evidence to have been written by Llaguno,[2] and which gives a somewhat different explanation of the changes in the 1789 text from the one given elsewhere.

In the *Vida*, Don Juan tells us that Luzán was working on a revised edition of the 1737 *Poetics* during his stay in Paris; that he was influenced in his thinking on the subject by associating with French poets and scholars there; and that he continued to collect material for his new edition by further reading.[3] Especially, it would seem, he read English poets, and, possibly, English critics, all of whom were far better known in Paris than in Madrid. Some years earlier the French Journal of Trévoux had observed that Luzán appeared not to know English writers.[4] Now, therefore, his son explains, Don Ignacio hoped to correct this inadequacy. And who more natural, we might add, than French intellectuals, just then becoming aware of the immensity of English possibilities, above all in the rational and psychological reaches of literature, who more natural than the Classically disposed French to act as Luzán's discriminating, international guides across the vastness of English literature? Consequently, where details are inserted about English writers in the 1789 edition, it seems reasonable to assume that Luzán himself was responsible for such additions, or at least for the notes from which new observations on English poets were developed. Milton, who figures prominently, was admired by French writers, especially in the first, the more Classical half of the eighteenth century. Alexander Pope, called "John" Pope by Luzán, who therefore can hardly have read him in the original, was also better known abroad in the first half of the period than in the second. By 1789 French interest had shifted to English writers outside Luzán's life-span. But all English references in both editions of the *Poetics* are such as would be encompassed within Luzán's own reading experience,[5] though he may have read English poetry in French translation.

In support of Luzán's direct authorship of the altered text, it transpires, from the Gayangos correspondence between Don Juan and Llaguno, that Luzán and Montiano had "worked together"[6] on the corrections and additions; that these had passed first into the keeping of Montiano, and only after his death into that of Llaguno. Don Juan originally had meant to bring out a complete edition of all his father's works, and his chief purpose in writing to Llaguno was to ask him to forward Luzán's notes so that they could be incorporated, as he would have wished, in the new version of the *Poetics* together with any relevant information about his life and offices. When Llaguno, after some prompting,[7] eventually replied,[8] agreeing to forward the corrected and augmented manuscript, he unequivocally stated that it contained the "original additions, which are of no small consideration for they include some entirely new chapters."[9]

This seems clear enough. Yet Llaguno's informal memorandum, written after the publication of the 1789 edition, is more than a little cryptic on the subject of the additions, and it has a warmly self-defensive air, as if, in response to some criticism about the new edition or his own part in it, he had been sufficiently provoked to assert his rights. In the context of his clarification he explains his relationship with Luzán. Don Eugenio had met the Preceptist as a young man and had been encouraged by him to practice the art of poetry and to develop wisely the talent which Luzán, Montiano, and others generously praised in Llaguno's youthful translation of Racine's *Athalie*. It was therefore, he says, in gratitude to Don Ignacio that he prepared the notes which Luzán had been making for an augmented edition of the *Poetics*, "putting them in order, adding to and touching up the weaker and undersized chapters."[10] This itself would be a task well within Llaguno's capacity. We know, from other sources, that Luzán discussed his opinions with his colleagues and friends, and Llaguno, who shared so many of the older scholar's sober tastes, and frequented the same literary company, must have been excellently equipped not only to arrange the notes, but to interpret them correctly.

A serious problem arises, however, from a further statement in the same memorandum. Llaguno expressly states, even, his tone and emphasis suggest, with a little asperity, that some of the new material in the 1789 edition had been contributed by himself, and that he had been willing for Luzán to receive credit for it despite the fact that he, Don Eugenio, could have used that material at some future time for projects of his own. His exact words are: "attributing to Luzán observations which in fact were my own and could have been used by me at a convenient time in the future." [11] Presumably those "observations" were of some extensiveness. Incidental remarks would hardly have served his personal designs for the future.

The National Library of Spain possesses a fragmentary set of manuscript notes by Llaguno entitled *Apuntes para la historia de la poesía (Notes for a History of Poetry),* some of which must have been written after 1746, for they refer to Luzán's poem on the festivities for Fernando VI's accession. Doubtless they formed part of a larger collection of memoranda. At times Llaguno appends personal reminders, referring himself to some other file *(cédula).* The notes comprise jottings on early and Renaissance Spanish poets, Spanish Preceptists, and some of the lesser-known Spanish dramas including the *Celestina,* which Llaguno mentions as being praised by a certain foreigner. In parenthesis he reminds himself to check the name of this foreigner. He mentions Luzán. First, in relation to the *Poetics,* he remarks:

"Luzán's *Poetics* has been justly praised here and in France. And the only defect that I can find in it is a certain redundance of style which (Luzán) acquired in Italy where he was brought up. He wrote an epic poem about the Proclamation of our King, a poem which pleased few people because it was so cold and full of commonplace *(humildes)* expressions" (8v).

Spaniards, of course, would have expected rhetoric where Luzán merely reasoned. The word "redundance" *(redundancia)* probably refers to Luzán's academic rather than idiomatic Castilian. More revealingly, Llaguno speaks of the Additions to Luzán's *Poetics.* A reminder to himself runs:

"On the beginnings of our drama, see Cervantes in his preface to his plays, and the end of *Don Quijote,* Part I, Nasarre in his Discourse on the plays, Luzán's Additions to the *Poetics*" (p. 82). Which must mean that he was using Luzán's notes for at least bibliographical purposes. Though on occasions he is evidently paraphrasing the *Poetics* of 1737, for instance, on poetic genius, to be discussed later:

". . . exaltation which carries them away and makes them say splendid things in such a manner that they seem changed into completely different persons" (p. 9. Cf. *Poetics*, 1737, p. 158).

Llaguno's statement about supplying observations of his own in the 1789 edition we have no reason in general to doubt. He would have a far deeper knowledge of Spanish literature than did Luzán, especially by 1789. He had talked with Luzán's intellectual companions, notably Montiano. He would know Luzán's intentions. He could add or subtract in accordance with Luzán's overall plan. Convincingly, intelligently, honorably, he could put his own words into Luzán's 1789 mouth. The trouble is that there are no external means of knowing exactly which of the additions were made originally by Don Ignacio and which were composed or arranged by Llaguno. About Montiano there is less difficulty. Any extra material for which he might have been responsible is probably not incorporated into the 1789 edition, since it was likely to have been concerned with acting and stage presentation, subjects in which Montiano was specializing between 1750 and 1753, and in which he must have interested Luzán sufficiently to inspire him to undertake that treatise on the Art of the Theater described by Don Juan as complementary to the *Poetics* and regrettably never developed.[12] Regrettable indeed is this unfulfillment. The results of rational discussions between two such perceptive scholars, coupled with Luzán's personal and practical observations of staging in Paris, would have given him an empiric advantage over all other modern Preceptists for some time to come.

As far as Llaguno is concerned, however, it is at least possible to make certain deductions from the internal evidence of the text itself. Let us recall that Llaguno had referred on one occasion to the addition of entire chapters made by Luzán to his 1737 text, and on another to the addition of parts of chapters supplied by himself. We suggest that both statements are readily acceptable. And if we are to credit some entire chapters to Luzán and other chapters, or parts of chapters, to Llaguno, it would seem logical to assign them by reasoning as follows:

First, there are five additional chapters to be taken into account in the 1789 text. In Volume I, a new chapter, 4, is inserted between the original Chapters 4 and 5 of Book I; it deals with Spanish popular poetry and the principles by which it was governed. Two supplementary chapters, 23 and 24, discuss verse forms and rhymes, including the ballad assonance or rhyming of vowels typical of Castilian poetry, and introduce lavish illustrations from Spanish literature. Near the beginning of Volume II are two more extra chapters, 2 and 3, on the history of Spanish drama, the second of which inserts, wholesale, the uninhibited *Arte nuevo de hacer comedias (New Art of Writing Drama)*, of 1609, written casually by Spain's master of carefree expression, Lope de Vega.

II *Additions and Alterations*

The new Chapter 4 of Volume 1 is patently intended to answer those who refute Neoclassical authority by arguing that rules are relative, that every country has a right to its own literary way of life, and that Spanish poets were neither ignorant nor uncultured but observed aesthetic laws of their own. This was an argument which Luzán must often have heard after 1737 and one which could not be admitted into his aesthetic philosophy. From his standpoint, if every nation were permitted to be a law unto itself, there would have been little reason throughout all these centuries for expounding Aristotelian *Poetics* to any nation but the Greeks: to him an unthinkable suggestion. No difficulty, therefore, is experienced in assigning the urgent expostulations of this chapter to Luzán himself. Emphatically and unshakably, like one who proclaims to pagans the revealed and unanswerable truth of monotheism, Luzán cuts dogmatically across the claims of multi-godhood. "There is only one *Poetics,* only one art of writing verse well, one that is common for the generality of all nations and for all times." [13]

Aesthetic ideas here are undoubtedly Luzán's, or such as he would have approved. If Llaguno's hand is to be suspected at all in this chapter, it may be imagined at work in management. Part of the material looks as if it had been merely transferred from notes. For instance, the long descriptions of the separate chapters of Encina's *Arte de trovar (Art of Versifying)*, are very notelike in their undeveloped summary and quotation. Possibly Llaguno, in order to give it coherence, had converted his friend's telegraphic material into linked sentences, and disposed it with rudimentary form and order. Finally, this chapter confusingly anticipates the additional Chapter 2 of Volume II; which looks like Llaguno's failure to coordinate two sets of notes, or, somewhat gratuitously, to have added examples and comments of his own wherever he found an opening for them.

Similarly, the additional Chapters 23 and 24 of the first volume are also roughly what we should expect of Luzán by 1754 and underline his matured sense of priorities: for instance, a warning to poets to subordinate meters to thought; an interest in Spanish ballad assonance, the medium through which Luzán had translated the couplets of *The Man of Modish Taboos;* a preoccupation with Italian usage; new illustrations as his reading developed from Spanish pre-Renaissance poets; a suggestion in Chapter 24 that a poet should select his rhyming words from nouns in preference to other parts of speech—a method practiced in the poetry of Luzán and not in that of Llaguno; an Italianate dislike of final stressed syllables, discussed by both Llaguno, in his *Notes* on poetry, and by Luzán, but with the latter's Italian training more in evidence.

So far, then, modifications of the 1737 text have been roughly what was to be expected. But the two extra chapters prefacing the second volume of the 1789 edition are less Luzán—like, in treatment, if not in content. Both deal with Spanish drama, its history and its popular principles. True, we are told in the *Vida* that Don Ignacio had been studying popular Spanish poets [14] whom, he seems to have discovered, he had underestimated. Passages from their works were meant, evidently, to be admitted into his text as additional illustrations of poetic virtues or defects, or simply of poetic experiments. But what we should not expect, at least in its 1789 form, is the addition at this point of a complete, uncritical chapter on the history of Spanish drama, followed by a further new chapter which, in discussing the attitude or principles of Spanish dramatists, quotes at full length the *New Art of Writing Drama* of Lope de Vega.

Luzán had a conspicuously good sense of proportion and organization. Yet, though there was reason in these two chapters to write more fully about Spain's Golden Age Preceptists whom playwrights had ignored, to include Spanish dramatists for wider illustration, to mention their divergences from the Classical and Neoclassical norm, to display scholarly knowledge of them and of their peculiarities, and to do them greater justice than had been done in 1737, there was no good reason to trace the entire history of Spanish drama here, least of all with fussy biographical detail, and with that headlong, disorderly rush of information reminiscent of the work of undergraduate examinees who are running out of time. The new chapters cannot be said to prove Luzán's Classical points even to a Classicist. They would, in fact, more suitably form a separate treatise; better still, Appendices. The likelihood is, therefore, that when Llaguno declared he could have used the material he attributed to Luzán for a publication of his own, he was referring to these two chapters, and that he had constructed this compendium-history of Spanish drama, basing it either wholly, or, more probably, in part, on Luzán's still unorganized and undeveloped notes.

Entire chapters apart, there are other small additions and alterations made in the body of the 1789 text, collectively important, in a few individual cases very significant, but too numerous for treatment in this short study. All of them are such as Luzán, critic and criticized in national Academies, would be likely to insert himself. Notably they represent his more extensive reading of Spanish writers, especially medieval poets, and his growing interest in staging and visual scenery. Certain individual items will be referred to where relevant in the following chapters.

CHAPTER 6

The Meaning of Authority

THE scholar's idea of what should constitute intellectual authority has changed from century to century. But over and above the little shifts of meaning, the little changes in adjustments and loyalties, one gathering force of intellectual change has divided off the last three centuries from all their predecessors. This is the change from an assumption that the best authority must be absolute, to a knowledge that no authority can be anything but relative.

Luzán, who by temperament was conservative, and yet who was not incapable of changing with the times, stood, only half-comprehendingly, just at that point in history where the uncertainties of practical scientists had begun to undermine the certainties of theoretic philosophers. It took him some time to realize that he might justifiably criticize those scholars established in his mind as lesser authorities. He never came to realize that those he regarded as ultimate authorities might also be open to dispute. Therefore his idea of the Spanish artist's rights of artistic freedom was bounded by his respect for traditional philosophers of countries which had specialized in aesthetic theory: notably Greece, Ancient Rome, Italy, and France.

I *Authority of the Ancients*

So when Luzán said that the "muses are free," [1] he meant that, in his opinion, they are free to do what they like within the civilized terms of a contract solemnized by academic authorities; as a man living in an autocracy is free to do what he likes in all unessentials so long as he conforms to state policy. The established academic lawgiver had been Aristotle. On his observations and interpretations of nature, man, and man's creative experience, the universities had based their codes and techniques of learning. Aristotle's cultural authority in intellectual schools of the eighteenth century had outlived his scientific preeminence. But his artistic creed, or what was thought to be his artistic creed, had, potentially, a specialist appeal for a century in search of scientific reasonableness. Aristotle's name was respected even by artists who disregarded his laws; as it had been respected by Lope de Vega and Calderón de la Barca. If the geniuses of Baroque Spain had never been attacked by those who advocated an Aristotelian literature of reason, it is very unlikely that Spaniards would have challenged either Luzán's codification of the Aristotelian *Poetics,* or the model tragedies based on this *Poetics.* The intelligent Spanish artist would have done what he had done before: he would have learnt at school, and in the university, the Aristotelian grammar of Rhetoric, and would unconcernedly have departed from it whenever his artistic intuition became stronger than the claims of his training. The Spaniards' respect for what they understand as authoritative, academic law and order has never been more than circumstantial, and, like the English, they have tended throughout their individualistic history to rely on law that is natively consuetudinary.

Luzán, therefore, in recalling his Spanish contemporaries to Aristotelian book was, as he meticulously explained, recalling them from consuetudinary to written standards of values. He must have seen himself, to some extent, as a kind of Muratori, the Italian Preceptist who, earlier in the century, had surveyed the excesses of an Italy then in decline and who, over the heads of unworthy imitators of the Baroque Marino and his followers, had called for a return to Aristotelian standards. Where Muratori blamed Marino, Luzán blamed the Spanish Góngora. The only differences in the two situations lay, first, in the fact that Spain had produced more eminent literary exponents of the Baroque than had Italy, and was more difficult to convince that any change was necessary; and secondly, in that Spanish dramatists, unlike their Italian contemporaries, could hardly be "recalled" to precedents never established. Besides, Spain, though politically united where Italy was divided, was much less amenable to organized campaigning. This does not mean, of course, that Italy and France might be expected to observe the letter of Aristotle's teaching indefinitely. What it means is that when new scientific reasoning, derived from new scientific experimentation, caused eighteenth-century French or Italian writers to depart from any letter of Aristotle's law, their shift of academic loyalties was in response to logic and practical calculation rather than to the prompting of accident, casual habit, or consuetudinary precedent. In other words, the task undertaken by Luzán was much more difficult than that undertaken by Muratori and required a different technique: a truth which Luzán in 1737 did not fully realize.

The chief, the most obvious, the most natural source of the teaching of both Muratori and Luzán was Aristotle to whom Don Ignacio occasionally refers in the original Greek. All other ancient and modern authorities used by Luzán, notably Horace and Italian and French Preceptists, to support his arguments were commentators and interpreters of Aristotle's aesthetic philosophy. They were scholars to whom the Spaniard went, as it were, to compare notes on the master's meaning, or on the best methods of organizing and modernizing Aristotle's implications.

It is important to remember, however, that even where Preceptists consulted their ultimate authority in Greek, they interpreted Aristotle's *Poetics* as simplified, organized, and dogmatized in Horace's *De Arte Poetica (Poetic Art)* and in later commentaries on both of these masters. Aristotle's more modern commentators, like S. H. Butcher, John Gassner, L. J. Potts, have widened and deepened our understanding of his aesthetic thought by restoring his *Poetics* to the context of his general philosophy— where it rightly belongs. The fact that Aristotle's original text is unfinished and fragmentary, largely in the form of notes—lecture notes, so it would seem—and that some of his ideas most difficult to grasp are inexplicit and undeveloped, has caused his whole meaning to be underestimated. Through the explicitness of Horace, and Horace's disciples, the Greek researcher's message was transformed. A recent critic poignantly described it as "one of the ironies of history that Aristotle's admirers from the sixteenth to the eighteenth century, should have tried to convert the explorer into an absolute lawmaker. It was their chief ambition, next to that of establishing themselves as legislators, too, by standing under the ample shadow of the great man's reputation." [2]

Certainly neither the modern interpreters of Aristotle whom Luzán often quotes—Paolo Beni, Ludovico Antonio Muratori, René Le Bossu—nor Luzán himself were universal enough in intellect or imagination to understand the full purport of a single aspect of Aristotle's philosophy. Scholarship was not yet sufficiently advanced or scientifically objective for sources and their contexts to be treated with full historical understanding. Greek, as a language and in its idiomatic peculiarities, was not known with as much detailed thoroughness as Latin, and the academic tendency was to translate Greek over-literally into inexact Latin approximations. Besides, it is always very difficult for the most realistic scholar to detach his mind from long established schools of thought; it is very easy to seize a few concrete illustrations in an obscure presentation of abstract ideas and build up a new, inaccurate coherence. We have to realize, therefore, that Luzán, like any other Aristotelian scholar of his times, saw Aristotle through intermediaries, that he underestimated the master's depth of thought, that he believed him to have been laying down rules of literary conduct, that, with a certain literalness which belonged to his epoch, he took the letter of such rules in strict obedience to a literary government wrongly called "Aristotelian," and that such rules represented to him, as to his colleagues, the basic requirements of law and order in the autocratic "republic" of letters. "Aristotelianism," for our purposes—which are the eighteenth-century purposes—must consequently be understood as a system of thought, believed by the Age of Reason to be the thought of Aristotle. Notwithstanding this, we should also remember that commentators had not been completely unaware of serious problems presented by Aristotle's original text. Luzán often uses his most intelligent discrimination in selecting, from among various possibilities, explanations nearest to practical reason and probability.

Individual problems inset in Aristotle's literary philosophy are best examined in relation to Luzán's direct or indirect interpretation of them in the corresponding chapters below. But as a general anticipation of the nature of the controversy which Aristotle's fragmentary *Poetics* provoked in his disciples, we should keep in mind the most obvious Aristotelian key words and phrases, largely concerned with drama, handed down as sacred, but interpreted out of context: words like *imitation, nature, unity, plot,* and ideas such as Aristotle's general assumption about the whole meaning and purpose of poetry, and his relation of poetry to philosophy.

Horace, whose *Poetic Art* was meant to do for Romans what Aristotle's *Poetics* had done for Greeks, was easier to understand because he spelled out the letter of certain ideas which Aristotle had left in the spirit. Being more superficial, and written in verse that beat into the memory, the *Poetic Art* provided scholars of aesthetics with certain catchphrases such as the "blending of profit and pleasure," "at once delighting and instructing . . ."[3] It reduced the meaning of creative "imitation" to imitation of the exterior habits, customs, and speech of men. It instructed playwrights on stage decorum and the desirability of converting ugly or violently realistic action into narration. It advocated the study of good models and disciplined method. It determined the length of the play in five acts and the reduction of characters on the stage. Perhaps most acutely, it specified that a poem must not only be intrinsically beautiful but pleasing, thereby introducing new sets of meditations and creating new schools of thought about the qualities needed within the Law to "please." Luzán, like his aesthetic companions, often found it convenient to call on Horace in support of his statements, particularly those concerning poetic appropriateness. Horace, however, had become even more trenchant than he originally was, through the dogmatic interpretations of his admirers—the French Preceptist, Boileau, for example—and those who discussed Horace's *Poetic Art* were often viewing it, at least partially, through somebody else's eyes. Frequently elaborations on Horace and elaborations on Aristotle unconsciously subordinated the meaning of the latter to the explicitness of the former.

On the other hand, some of Aristotle's Italian and French commentators occasionally gave to one or another of the problems arising from his obscurity or incompleteness an original interpretation of philosophical value. Luzán evidently was deeply interested in all reasonable, new possibilities of interpretation and in the problems which those possibilities in their turn produced. These occasions, and they are frequent, show that Luzán was anything but passive in his study of the meaning of authorities. Over the years he did not change his general Classical stand. But his *Poetics* is not merely comprised of imitation, quotation, and adulation. It is primarily a discussion, just as his treatises on ancient authorities before the Academy of History are discussions, of varied possibilities, some of which teased his intellect creatively. Nor did Luzán ignore the views of creative writers, least of all where these could bring practical experience to bear on academic theory. He was prepared, for example, to concede several points to Corneille on the stretching of the Unities. Probably the Frenchman's caustic remark that he was ready to observe the theorists' logic in all its niceties when someone had put these niceties into practice and produced better artistic results than he, struck Luzán as good common sense.[4]

For his part Corneille, even within the Classical tradition, was inclined, consciously or unconsciously, to make theory fit the practical fact of his stage success. Genius is baffling to all but genius in its inability to disbelieve in itself. Its trust ultimately is in insubstantial vision, not in niceties of procedure. The man with perfect musical pitch does not reach the required note by normal musical ways. The linguist with a musical "ear" trusts more to his musical instinct than to rules of phonetics and intonation, though rules may help him incidentally. The man with psychological insight uses his reason, but takes astonishingly unconventional shortcuts. So, it would seem, genius is made self-confident by its possession of the mysterious perfect pitch of artistry. Aristotle apparently realized that fact and was tormented enough by the phenomenon to try to analyze it scientifically from the examples of Greek drama that he knew. His disciples were not goaded by the same challenge. They did not seem to perceive it. But some of them, Luzán included, were discerning theatergoers or readers of drama, and could understand that practitioners were not entirely dependent on theory. Corneille might explain or defend himself. But he did not deny himself. And it is interesting that Luzán found this attitude, in Corneille at least, not unreasonable, for the Frenchman could demonstrably create his own illusion in a quiet and inconspicuous way. So long as this was a broadly Classical way, Luzán was ready to concede to the dramatist the right to employ individual means to suit his Classical ends. Perhaps to some small extent Luzán was even beginning by 1754 to realize that Lope de Vega's undeniably successful practice, too, might be, if not approved, at any rate respected. But the Luzán of 1754 would still be unable to imagine Lope as an artistic rival to Corneille.

II *Authority of the Moderns*

Investigation of Luzán's Italian and French authorities is the aspect of his *Poetics* which has been most thoroughly examined.

The modern Preceptists discussed by Luzán, and to whom we shall refer incidentally when occasion offers, are very conveniently listed for researchers, with statistics as to the number of times each writer is mentioned in the *Poetics,* by Dr. Sebold.[5] His statistical analysis in part confirms what had already been argued by Dr. Juan Cano: [6] that Luzán used Italian Preceptists more than French. Additionally it stresses the fact, not before given sufficient importance by those who have tried to prove Luzán's dependence either on French or on Italian theorists, that the predominant influence is of Aristotle directly, with Horace in second place, and that the second edition of Luzán's *Poetics* shows increased reference to the basic authority of these two. As for Luzán's consciousness of foreign modern Preceptists, Dr. Sebold's statistics and his fully annotated Bibliography prove that the first four in numerical importance are the Italian Paolo Beni, the French Le Bossu, the Italian Ludovico Antonio Muratori, and the French playwright Pierre Corneille.

Of these authorities on whom Luzán draws frequently for suggestions, Paolo Beni is a commentator who used a Latin version of Aristotle with which Luzán would be familiar.[7] The rest are Preceptists who also base their views on Aristotle as the ultimate authority, but who have views of their own, critical, interpretative, analytical, or imaginative, in which Luzán was specially interested. Le Bossu, for example, he consulted on the difficult meaning of the word *fabula* and the organization of plot.[8] Muratori, when dealing with Aristotle's meaning of "nature," had arranged the different faces of nature into classifications which Luzán borrowed.[9] Corneille on several questions—notably the Unities and the attitude of audiences—supplied Luzán with various practical conclusions.[10]

But these, if the most important of Luzán's authorities, are, Dr. Sebold shows, a mere four out of some eighty-eight different writers—largely Classical, Italian and French—mentioned in the first edition, and 105 in the second. In this respect and as an overall assessment of Luzán's use of his sources, three final facts should be kept in mind. First, that Luzán normally goes out of his way to refer to his authorities. Even, it may be said, he takes a scholarly pride in welcoming them, as it were, to a Preceptist conference. So that the charges of imitation and of unoriginality fall rather foolishly to the ground. For Luzán's intention was not to set up an aesthetic system in opposition to that of anyone else, but to integrate the best aesthetic ideas he knew into a well-organized, practical philosophy. This is the sense of his introductory words, "full, perfect, and complete treatise on Poetics," [11] describing his own project. He was not really so self-satisfied that he thought his own *Poetics* better than that of any of his foreign predecessors. Emphatically he would never have dared to try to improve on Aristotle. What his words "full, perfect, and complete" mean in their context is that his modern *Poetics* was offered as a work of scholarship fully documented to date.

Secondly, we should notice from Dr. Sebold's charts that while in the course of the two editions Luzán's references to his many authorities increase, the preponderance of ancient over modern, and Italian over French authorities remains constant: a positive indication indeed of where Luzán's modern preferences instinctively lay, with the Italians.

Lastly, let it be said that the most notable increase between 1737 and 1789 within any one class of source-nationalities, is in the Spanish sector. Part of the reason for this we know already, part of it will be examined in due course. Broadly viewed, however, it is the aspect of the *Poetics* giving the strongest sign of realistic life. Of the Spaniards, too, the least relevant to Luzán's direct purpose is the most influential: Benito Jerónimo Feijoo. Luzán occasionally mentions him, always admiringly. But infinitely more important than direct reference to him is Luzán's imitation of Feijoo's realistic methods of reasoning, of his vigorous thrust through ambiguities, of his imaginative flights; while the essential proof of Feijoo's influence may be concretely observed in certain verbal reminiscences detailed in relevant chapters below. Feijoo was by far the healthiest modern influence on the Aragonese scholar, for the constructive reason that he taught Don Ignacio to think for himself. Authority can have no nobler meaning.

CHAPTER 7

The Poetics. *Book I.*
Philosophical Orientation

THE *Poetics,* in both versions, is divided into four Books of unequal length, the first and third of which are rather more significant for the history of literary controversy than the second and fourth. Book I attempts a philosophical assessment of the nature of poetry, based not only on what Luzán, by authority, believed, but what he personally understood. It arranges some of the principles scattered fragmentarily about Aristotle's *Poetics* into coherent order and analyzes their significance. It provides essential evidence of the way in which Luzán's mind speculatively operated. Book III, on Drama, is the best known because it is the most controversial of the four. Drama was the only area in which Don Ignacio was obliged seriously to challenge Spanish tradition, in which, consequently, he was mentally stretched to his full capacity. The other two sections, a long Book II on the Lyric, Book IV on the Epic, also discuss a number of general questions which might have figured better in Book I. But on the whole, they are more concerned with practical illustration. One of Luzán's sponsors, Father Miguel Navarro, of the University of Zaragoza, when enumerating the virtues of the *Poetics,* astounds modern readers by giving pride of place to its method of classification. The entire work had pleased him, he says, "but, above all, the division of the four Books and the subdivisions of so many and such unusual chapters." [1] His judgment would be specially appropriate in relation to that lengthy Book II.

I   A *full, perfect, and complete treatise on Poetics*
(Luzán, *Poetics,* I, 1.)

Courteously, and for the most part dispassionately, Luzán begins by addressing himself to Spaniards' sense of unease at the idea of unfamiliar rules and regulations, to Spaniards' impatience with formal constriction. He may not have known that their objection has never been to artistic rules as such, for those who might want to observe them, but to a categorical commitment with rules and to the thought of rule-enforcement in all circumstances. Possibly he did realize, however, that, in the eighteenth century, a distaste for detailed commitment in literature ran parallel to, even to a certain extent reflected, the country's unease at the elaborate officialdom of the French House of Bourbon recently ascended to the Spanish throne. At all events he makes much initially of the fact that the rules and regulations he presents in the *Poetics* are not his own, not new, not arbitrary, not in the usual sense foreign, but go back some two thousand years to an authority widely known and widely accepted; that they are founded on common reason, and that, like all that is founded on reason, are as venerably old as reason itself.[2]

An appeal to reason is always disarming. Designed to enlist the cooperation of those who consider themselves to be men of intelligence, it can not merely challenge, but intimidate. Reason, too, was the key word of the century and was equated with superior understanding. Luzán was not without dialectic intuitiveness. However, he was not sufficiently ahead of his times to understand that a rationalized, official acceptance of some version of the Classical ideal need not necessarily imply that nonconformist literature was substandard. Nor was Luzán, or any Neoclassical Preceptist, imaginative enough to construct a *Poetics* noncomparatively. Like Antonio Nebrija who made the first grammar of the Spanish language by noting similarities and differences between Spanish and Latin parts of speech, Luzán judges Spain's Golden Age by the way in which it measures or fails to measure up to his codification of the Classical ideal. French and Italian writers, always very comfortable, for some national reason, in their Classical element, had developed a habit of drawing odious comparisons when judging literatures unlike their own. And Luzán, for all his intelligence, was, by circumstance and training, too dependent on the standard of values of French and Italian scholars invariably to see things unobstructed by their prejudices. Consequently, the *Poetics* is sent on its way with provocative warnings that Don Ignacio, that least belligerent of men, is no respecter of Golden Age persons. Even Luzán's qualified approval of the Golden Age masters would just then have been better left unspecified. Had Lope de Vega united study and art to his natural ability, thought Luzán, who had no idea how cultured a man Lope de Vega really was, Spanish dramas might have been the envy of other nations. Instead of which, he tactlessly insisted, Spanish dramas are generally the object of other nations' "criticism and laughter." [3] How sad it was, reflected Don Ignacio, single-mindedly pursuing the topic, that when much could have been done to stop the literary rot, virtually nothing was attempted. So the erecting of a Poetics-barrier against the onrush of decadence Luzán considered to be his special task. It should be remarked that, apart from additional names of Spanish Preceptists, his statement on the Golden Age in the 1789 version remains as it provocatively stood. A gentle and modest scholar he may have been. But he had the courage of his convictions.

II *First Essay in Philosophy*

Though the main purpose of the first few chapters of the *Poetics* is to prepare a way through Spain's habits of thought for the infiltration of literary authoritarianism and to make ready for an analysis of the essence of poetry by tracing the intellectual and popular origins of this form of art (Chaps. II–IV), Luzán, at the outset, points firmly towards his distant goal, to the ultimate value of what he believed to be right aesthetic thinking. The first Aristotelian principle to emerge appears within the first few lines and makes a stylistically effective opening to Chapter I:

"The prerogatives of poetry are well known . . . whether with regard to its purpose which is the same as that of Moral Philosophy, or with regard to the means by which poetry has the advantage of all the other arts and sciences and even of Philosophy itself; for, as Horace says, poetry teaches the same maxims as philosophy, but in a better and more efficacious way." [4] This is a version of Aristotle's "Poetry, therefore, is a more philosophical and higher thing than history" [5] and, apparently, of Horace's ". . . . daring eloquence brought with it unheard-of language, and sayings filled with useful maxims, with prophetic foresight, rivaled the pronouncements of the oracle of Delphi." [6]

Despite the dignity lent to his *Poetics* by the tone of such an opening, however, Luzán is taking too soon for granted a generalized summary of something not yet discussed, not indeed ever discussed in all its complexity, and he is giving too superficial an impression of something which can only be understood in its profundity. In Aristotle the philosophical nature of poetry is projected by his argument before he mentions the word "philosophical" at all. It is anticipated by his analysis of the art of re-creating, on a scale larger than life, the vital functioning of mental and physical cause and effect, and is stated just after he has begun to distinguish between what is lifelike in fact and what can be accepted as such. Aristotle's illuminating presentation of poetry as philosophical is therefore an equivalent, perhaps, of Wordsworth's universal awareness as a poet, of being able to "see into the life of things." [7] On this as on many occasions when he is freed from his Neoclassical commentators, and read in more than isolated phrases, Aristotle emerges as a timeless thinker absorbed in the reality of process.

Luzán, together with French and Italian Classicists, takes Aristotle's conclusion as an accepted dogma, omitting the previous process of reasoning, and losing his reader's active cooperation thereby. Nor does he here experience the need, as on some important occasions, to compare notes with other commentators. He has nothing further to say on the subject throughout this Book except to repeat himself in a concluding chapter whose title heading, "On the Purpose of Poetry," is more interesting than its contents. The truth was that to Luzán and his Neoclassical authorities the "philosophical" nature of poetry meant only that poetry, as an aesthetic commentary on human experience, could pleasingly expound and exemplify moral truths: the beauty of moral goodness, the tragedy of moral wrongmindedness. By "philosophy" is understood "moral philosophy," by "poetic art," a vehicle of moral utility. In the *Iliad*, points out Luzán, dissension among the Greek captains illustrates the political dangers of disaccord: in the *Odyssey*, the adventures of Ulysses demonstrate the danger to the state of the prolonged absence of a Prince. The emphasis has shifted. Somewhere in the Neoclassical debates the idea of the philosophical element in poetry as the mountain peak of superior understanding has been lost. The "philosophy" discussed by Luzán and his kind is a moral instruction of the plains. Ungarnished philosophy could even be harmful to those who did not understand it, reflected Luzán. Indeed, so it might; but not in the complex, larger sense in which the concept was being used by Aristotle.

Given these initial simplications and reductions which Luzán made in good Neoclassical company, we can more easily understand how other intangibles of poetic mystique could be converted into commonplaces.

III   *The Crucial Principle of "Imitation"*

Having dispensed with the foregoing preliminaries, Luzán, in Chapter V, "plunges" into the deepest aesthetic problems set by Aristotle, in full knowledge of their difficulties and of their basic importance. What constitutes the essence of Poetry, and in what sense may poetry be said to share with other arts the function of "imitating nature"? Don Ignacio pauses for an instant, it would seem, to take stock of the enormity of these problems before proceeding. "Now is the time," he observes, resorting, under the momentousness of the occasion, to a Classical simile, "when, like one who has left the shore and who puts out to sea with sails unfurled, we plunge into the deep waters of our subject." [8]

Seldom did Luzán resort to poetic style in academic treatises. But not only by his simile do we know that he has recognized the auspiciousness of this occasion. Presently, by a comparison of their definitions, he will expose the fundamental perplexity of his chosen authorities on these tremendous questions. More significant, from our point of view, is the disclosure that he remains dissatisfied with all their definitions, and that he finds himself obliged to supply a composite definition of his own based on the most convincing suggestions he has studiously collected. Even then he is far from convinced that the matter has been settled. At the beginning of Chapter VI, "On Imitation," he is still brooding over the prospect of deep difficulty, repeating himself as he somewhat distractedly surveys the many possibilities of alternative courses, and eventually deciding to stop to define the crucial word *imitation*, "since on this word depends our understanding of the whole subject." [9]

First, however, in Chapter V he had tried to rationalize the mystery of the "essence" of poetry. Remembering, presumably, Aristotle's use of the word "maker" with respect to the producer of different kinds of meter, Luzán explains that a poet is a "maker" or "creator," that poetry, by its very etymology, is in essence an "invention" or "fiction" (*fábula*), and "denotes that faculty . . . of giving soul and sense to inanimate things and creating, as it were, a new world." [10] It will be noticed that already by using the words "giving . . . to inanimate things" he is committing himself to a narrower interpretation of "invention" than he must. Nevertheless, his choice of creativeness as the basic character of poetry is well judged. A new world, fashioned by a man's own imagination, is the work of an artist, and if such an artist expresses himself in meter, which Luzán, despite misgivings, considered necessary to true poetry, he is a poet and his work is poetry. At the outset Luzán had recognized a motorquality. Some of his authorities had not. Muratori, for instance, had described the essence of poetry more vaguely as the imitation or depicting of truth, something "presented to the eyes of the soul" as a parallel to what is seen "by the eyes of a painter." [11]

However, it is not until he begins to explain how a poet's inventive faculty essentially functions that Luzán truly enters the deepest waters. In the *Poetics*, Aristotle had described poetry as "a mode of imitation" and the objects of imitation as "doings," according to Potts's rendering, [12] or "men in action" according to Butcher's. [13] In his *Physics*, Aristotle had stated that "Art imitates nature," meaning, prompts Butcher, with the full text in his hands, that "art imitates the method of nature," or "catches hints from nature" to achieve "the union of matter with constitutive form." [14] From their wide philosophical and scientific context, these terms "imitate" and "nature" had been transferred by the less philosophical Horace to the reduced, aesthetic confines of his recommendation: "I would advise the well-instructed imitator to take his model from life and customs." [15] They were then codified by commentators of both Aristotle and Horace to form the well-known and ill-understood principle that poetic art "imitates nature"— "imitates," now, in the sense, not of copying techniques, but of copying the finished, external results, of copying not activity and process, but end products. Plato's looking glass had mirrored precisely these end products of life, [16] and his idea had passed into verbal currency. In England the phrase culturally circulated as art "holds the mirror up to the nature."

Understanding this general idea in its narrowest, its most literal, nonphilosophical and nonscientific sense, the Neoclassicist usually believed, all too wrongly, that, when he repeated it, he was stating a self-evident truth as deep as Aristotelian seas. Luzán, under the guidance of certain of his modern authorities, might sometimes suspect that "imitation of nature" or "imitation of real life" had more to do with extraordinary vision than with ordinary sight. But both they and he had been taught to concentrate so closely, with such automatic reverence, on the apparent letter of Aristotelian law that they never quite perceived its spirit or re-related it to its full context, and did not sufficiently test, from their own experience of the power or the entrancement of poetry, the technical meaning either of "nature" or of "imitation." To them, therefore, "imitation of nature," at its broadest, meant a decorously selective copy, reproduction, or, more imaginatively, re-creation of external life as this was normally understood in unscientific terminology. We must stress that the last is Neoclassical interpretation at its broadest. A narrower interpretation of "real life" by Antonio Minturno and discarded by Luzán, confined the poet to imitating the life of people to the exclusion of other objects. Luzán, usually on the side of the liberals, chooses to follow the version of Paolo Beni, whom often he prefers, on grounds of comprehensiveness, to more limited authorities. Beni's theory is closer to Aristotle in its use of the significant word "action" which we shall have cause to discuss more fully later. It runs as follows: ". . . imitation, at some length, of an action, which, giving great pleasure to men, animates them and incites them to virtue and to a happy, well-ordered life." [17]

Even now Luzán still finds the definition too constrictive, especially in its specification of "length" and "action," and, taking more eclectic surveys, he produces a composite improvement which increases the poetic potentialities of nature by admitting it to the abstract reaches of the universal: ". . . imitation of nature either in a universal or a particular sense, in verse, for the purpose of utility, or for pleasure, or for both." [18] Because "things," insists Don Ignacio, can be imitated as they are in themselves (particular) or as they are in people's ideas and opinions, the last being his conception of what is "universal."

Nevertheless Luzán, like all Neoclassical Preceptists and all Spanish Neoclassical playwrights, if not lyricists, saw the principle of the imitation of nature as two-dimensional only. That is, he saw it as the copying of external end products: whether physical, natural objects, like man and beasts; or man's words,

the logically deduced expression of his presumed feelings, sentiments, and thoughts; or his actions as the invaryingly calculable
exteriorization of his words. That is to say, he saw the length
and breadth of form, and left the intangibilities of poetic power
still unexplained. What none but Aristotle had ever allowed for,
was that invisibly unifying technique, the life or motor-dimension
of actual process which, incidentally, by a logical development of
Aristotelian thinking, could generate the realistic atmosphere of
mental pressures. No wonder Luzán found the problem of definition so tormenting. He had been carried away by great poetry. He
knew a little about writing poetry at first hand. Yet he appears
to be unaware that he could not put his finger on a poem's life-
source. Admittedly he does make a certain stand, more Aristotelian than Neoclassical, against the tyranny of narrowly interpreted "utility" as the ultimate aim of a poem. Horace had
chiefly favored a combination of the two purposes: utility and
pleasure. But Luzán stresses that pleasure alone may be admitted
as a rightful purpose of poetry, so long as pleasure does not
offend social and religious custom. Pleasure in itself, runs his
argument, is a form of utility, "the utility of a legitimate and
honest entertainment." [19] In the 1789 text, Luzán extends his
tolerance on this score to embrace the idea that if verse were not
essential to poetry, as in fact he feels it should be, he would be
inclined to include as poetry splendid passages of prose—nowadays we should call them purple passages—descriptions written,
for instance, he remembered, by historians who, with well-in-
formed imagery and inventiveness, could re-create an ancient
scene. Luzán was thinking at the time, he said, of instances in
Livy.[20]

Aristotle's idea of imitation was much more dynamic than that
of any of his commentators and would account for the spirit and
essence of all purple passages as opposed to their organization.
Thus it is all the more ironic that the fragmentary nature of his
notes should have misguided his early commentators. Since Luzán
and some of Luzán's immediate authorities continue to show that
they are tormentingly aware of Aristotle's inaccessibility, it is
necessary to remind ourselves of what they all failed to see.

In the first place, as Butcher clarifies, Aristotle's phrase "Art
imitates nature" from its context in the *Physics*, and from reference to "imitation" and "nature" in other Aristotelian treatises,

will not support the simple interpretation that art is a "bare imitation," a "literal transcription of the world of reality," [21] or as
perhaps we might say now, a photographic copy. In the *Physics,*
we are told, Aristotle was not drawing any distinction between
useful art and fine arts, and his scientifically directed conception
of "nature" was not of its external appearance or an end product,
but "the creative force," the "productive principle of the universe,"
or as another commentator puts it, the "embodying another nature
and acting under the domination and control of its force." [22] The
meaning of the problematic term "imitation," then, would seem
to be made problematic by modern terminological ambiguity and
by the different kinds of emphasis that the word "nature" can
admit. Aristotle's emphasis is on the urgent activity of forces
as real, yet as ultimately invisible, as the force of life itself. The
emphasis of new Classicists is on the exteriorized, even material
result of that activity: the photograph. Their own analogy was
usually with painting. On this change of emphasis much of the
life-energy in poetry is left completely unaccounted for. Simpli-
fying Butcher, we might say that Aristotle's emphasis is on the
origin, development, and process of complex motive forces which
are exteriorized in activity. Aristotle had explained that the fine
arts imitate "men in action," a reference, pursues Butcher, whose
translation this is, to all fine arts and not merely dramatic and
narrative poetry where "action" is more obviously represented, a
reference, in fact to activity of mental life and personality, "all
that constitutes the inward and essential activity of the soul." [23]
Here was a reality beside which Luzán's poetic "new world" [24]
created by the imagination looks like a world of ghosts.

It was no wonder that literal eighteenth-century Preceptists
should sometimes have been troubled in their Aristotelian loyalties when they compared what they understood to be Aristotle's
words with apparently unrealistic Greek practices accepted in all
naturalness by the Philosopher: for instance, the Greek use of the
Chorus to which Aristotle takes no exception, and the allusion in
French or Italian drama to anachronistic pagan gods and sentiments. Admittedly, a modern Preceptist had good reason, given
the circumstances prevailing in his times, for assuming that
Chorus, pagan gods, and pagan sentiments were better left to
earlier epochs. For he was incapable of understanding that the
Greek Chorus, which Aristotle insisted must be fully integrated

into the action, was the representation of an inner reality of atmospheric pressure; or that when used by an author of imagination, and cooperative actors, pagan sentiments could be as true to life in atmosphere, if not in actuality, as anything or anyone photographically realistic. Still, from the Aristotelian standpoint, Luzán's illustrations are too sensory, too concrete. Quoting from Monsignani, he commits himself to the belief that poetic excellence consists in representing concepts so well, so closely, "with such inventiveness and clarity that the understanding does not merely read them but can see them." [25] Emphasis lies heavily on the word "see." Moreover, when Monsignani goes on to distinguish between two possible "forms" of imitation—that is, indirect or inventive imitation, and direct, or actual imitation, Luzán busies himself with concrete developments of Monsignani's distinction, explaining that inventive imitation is usually concerned both with "human actions"—an Aristotelian idea used in its most superficial and external sense—which have not taken place, but which, Luzán's meaning is, are based on lifelike behavior in lifelike circumstances, and with actual imitation of existing objects. We should notice, by the way, that although Luzán was thinking almost exclusively of external nature, a fact becoming more evident as the *Poetics* proceeds, he was not thinking of a static nature. "Because," summarizes Luzán, introducing another Aristotelian key concept, to occupy us later, "because, while inventive imitation re-creates an action so verisimilar that it looks true to life, actual imitation infuses into things such movement and spirit that they look not only true, but alive." [26]

The fundamental question of verisimilitude will be seen to preoccupy Luzán extensively in later chapters of the *Poetics*. But its introduction here as the cornerstone of his conception of art cannot be overstressed. Again he is led away from interior subtleties of so promising a philosophical subject by the practical details supplied by modern Preceptists as clarifications. Muratori, surveying the whole range of objects which an artist might justifiably use as objects of imitation, had classified them under three headings or "worlds": the celestial world of objects, that is, lacking body and matter, like God, angels, souls, etc; the human world of men with rational souls; and the nonhuman world of nature. To the tidy mind of Luzán, Muratori's three-world system was understandably satisfying.

In fact, it was too satisfying. For while he is careful to point out that the three-world system, in addition to covering things perceived by the senses, admits things which can only be perceived by the understanding, like spiritual truths and the things combined of matter and spirit, or the misunderstood Aristotelianism "human actions," yet he demonstrates the limitedness, perhaps the necessary limitedness, of new Classicists by assuming that the "world" of "human actions" is merely one of three classes of subject matter. In Aristotle's philosophy the phrase comprehensively referred to all that could be understood and encompassed within human mind and mental activity, within human life; that is, not so much the human story as the human technique. It is very noticeable that when classifications like Muratori's are made for the convenience of the nonphilosopher, the spiritual "world" covering God, the soul, and moral and religious teaching about spiritual things, is thought of as didactic illustration, not as an aspect of higher mental experience. Again, then, the gap between Aristotle and those who acknowledged his authority is seen to widen. His disciples knew that they did not fully understand his every detail and put down their difficulties to the fragmentary state of the master's lecture notes—as if, for example, "human actions" were only part of a larger explanation of all the objects of imitation he might eventually have specified: themes about God and spiritual ideas; themes about human actions and thoughts; lyrical themes describing nature scenery. Their mistake was to strive for classifications where they should have looked for inner relationships. Aristotle does refer in due course to themes and subject matter. But when speaking of "doings," or "men in action," he is not ingenuously concerned with a category of objects, with different kinds of themes about what men do, or think, or say, but with the activity of mind itself, with will and creative forces, with the inner energy of motives and the outer, universal application of inner cause and effect.

IV *The Principle of Universality*

The figure of speech initially used by Luzán, the image of the ship setting out for the deep seas, was much more appropriate than he knew. Neoclassical ships sailed over the real Aristotelian mysteries and did not, like individual divers, literally plunge into them. Nowhere is this truer than in Luzán's discussion of the Aristotelian principle of universality in Chapter VIII, where he tries to distinguish between imitation of nature in particular objects and imitation of nature on a universal plane. Remembering the charts of Plato and Aristotle, and with his eye on other aesthetic mariners, Horace among them, Luzán finds that to explain the imitation of the particular, as imitation of objects as they really are, is by far the lesser of his two difficulties. His unilluminatingly roundabout description of universal imitation tells how objects appear to be "in that universal idea which we form of things, the which idea comes to constitute a kind of original or type from which individual or particular objects are copies." [27]

This does not take Neoclassicists philosophically very far and Luzán is intelligent enough to know it. He seems chiefly disturbed by being obliged, as he supposes, to presume that a universal quality in a dramatic character—the virtue of courage, for instance—is a perfect abstract of courage free from humanly imperfect motives like fear, temerity, anger, or desire for vengeance; that universal beauty—of Helen of Troy, for example—is the sum total, as it were, of all characteristics of beauty taken from beautiful but individually imperfect women. Poetic perfection of this sort would make very dull stage characters, one would think. Looking in his academic way for evidence, however, he remembers examples of distinguished men in history who fulfilled this requirement of universal courage, and he feels able to disagree with the Italian theorist, Gian Vincenzo Gravina, by maintaining that imitation of the universal is not exclusively a poetic ideal, meaning, presumably, that there do exist true originals of ideal behavior and character.

All this misses the point. What Aristotle meant by "universal" was not concerned with a mere archetype or abstract, least of all with a collection of superlative qualities. It was concerned, interprets Butcher, taking as usual the whole of the Aristotelian context into account, with the "manifestation of a higher truth." [28] And, here, the concept "higher" has little to do with Platonic belief that a disembodied moral ideal is higher than a good individual's moral act. "Higher" is being used, we think, in the sense that some aspect of experience, common to all humanity, has been perceived and illuminated by a superior understanding.

This "manifestation of a higher truth," this relating of, for instance, a character on the stage to the stream of timeless human experience, the powerful destruction of the barriers between particular characters and audiences of any race or time, the breaking down of the separate compartments into which each of a series of acts or incidents is individualized, has been consistently demonstrated by the world's artistic masters. If, instead of regarding "universality" as the formal "ideal," "message," or moral lesson of a literary masterpiece, important though some such message may be as a separate consideration, we think of it as the entire human impact made on us by that masterpiece, we could say that "universality" in, for example, the Spanish *Celestina,* is the author's superior perception of how one mind must work when it is dominating another: a perception not easily acquirable by everybody. Universality is expressed as the human strain of a guilt complex through the guilt complex of Orestes in Aeschylus' *Choephoroe* or *Eumenides;* as the nervous atmosphere of resistance to materialist reasoning through Sophocles' *Antigone;* as the fever-inducing climate of ambition in *Macbeth* or in Racine's *Britannicus.* In all of these instances the operative obsession for the spectator is no conventional, bookish, or pedagogic abstraction, but a living force into which, by possessing certain smaller qualities of it in his own chemistry, every member of the universe can appreciatively enter.

But regarded more narrowly by Neoclassicists as a purely moral ideal, the universal quality in literature was normally thought to act as the generalizing agent of elucidation in allegories about good and evil: universal moral summary as opposed to universal imitation. For this reason polemic arose about which would be more "useful" to society, the imitation of idealized, universal models or the imitation of particular individuals, who perhaps were beginning to appeal more to eighteenth-century rationalism. Since the Greek word for poetry had had connections with "doing" or "making," some authorities, like Plato, evidently doubted if a poet ought to concern himself with themes that he had not invented. Others thought that fiction should be altogether omitted. Again, this is nearly all beside the Aristotelian point. Luzán, who mentions such differences of opinion, was narrowing the distinction between particular and universal to the difference between fact and fancy. It will be remembered that the early sixteenth-century Spanish playwright, Torres Naharro, divided his dramas into two categories: "Plays about ordinary life" or *comedias a noticia,* and plays on fictitious subjects, or *comedias a fantasía.* The last word, *fantasía,* is adopted from Plato and used by Luzán in the way in which Naharro used it. There was a tendency among Preceptists to equate these two categories, realistic and fictitious or idealistic, with the particular and the universal respectively.

In the reduced area of this controversy, Luzán took a typically commonsense line. He might not see the full implication of Aristotle's aesthetic vision. Yet, warned by common observation, he hesitated to ally himself with one of the two narrow schools of "realistic" and "fictitious" adherents. Faced with such widely differing opinions, he therefore felt it was best to follow a middle way. And, if this seems an undramatic solution, it is at least the kind of solution on which scholarly liberalism is based. We should not underrate him on this or any other critical occasion.

Even had Plato not already been mentioned, Luzán's statement that all art should be subordinated to the state political, and therefore the public good, would have shown that the principles of the *Republic* loomed large at the back of his thought. Not only, he explains, is it necessary to illumine a spectator's understanding with the light of truth, and dispose it to what is good and right, but it is also necessary to win over his will and move it to practice the truth which it has learned and the right which it has now recognized. If this seems to indicate a bleak world of art, the Neoclassicists did not think so. Their idea of the pleasure to be derived from universals was related to that incidental ornamentation by means of which moral truth was to be made attractive. For which reason, Luzán, to his own way of thinking, is explaining the whole force of Aristotle's statement on the philosophical value of poetry by saying that poetry, which teaches pleasurably, is, for that very reason, more powerful than any other method of teaching and informing. He actually goes to the practical extreme—which his contemporaries would undoubtedly approve—of comparing the poet's method of teaching universal truths with the method of administering medicine by means of coating the rim of the medicine glass with sugar:

"Oh, if Aristotle were to come to life again," exclaimed Herder, "and could see the false and absurd use to which his rules have been put . . . !" [29]

In order to substantiate his ideas about universals, Luzán significantly points to the works of Metastasio. This certainly was a librettist of high operatic standing, a writer warm and lyrically vital, often intuitive. But Metastasio's heroes usually portray a ready-made integrity which turns them into symbols of perfection and which, instead of universal vision, suggests short-sightedness. If Preceptists could be content with second-rate tragedy of this kind for the sake of the "perfect" characteristics and the imaginative language, then we have clear enough proof, were other proof lacking, that such Preceptists were not thinking on the true Aristotelian plane or on the plane of the best Greek practice.

To Luzán, however, Metastasio's characters were examples illustrating the social value of poetic "universals." More, there would be actual danger, he solemnly believed, in depicting average men with average virtues and defects, for ignorant audiences would be liable to confuse good with bad. Undeniably, virtues and defects in master tragedies often do merge, and whether we see that effect as desirable or not depends on our idea of the purpose of poetry. Luzán had made his own position, which is that of his century, thoroughly clear. If poetry could not be seen, from every angle, to serve primarily and unmistakably the interest of public morals, its pleasing qualities were invalid. Like that of the dramatic Unities, this was a principle which could be widely held because it was so easy to understand. Any good argument against it would involve psychological subtleties which were not taught in Perceptists' textbooks and were as yet known only to artistic intuition.

So, again misunderstanding Aristotle, Luzán adopts the principle ascribed to Sophocles—certainly a more eminent authority than Metastasio—of not imitating what is, but "what ought to be" [30] in a moral sense too, and he is much exercised in trying, as a matter of orthodoxy, Platonic and Christian, to prove that by representing what "ought to be," the perfection of the Creator's world is not being called into question. The poet must not imagine, Luzán is careful to insist, that he can meddle with what the Creator has already perfected in the original makeup of all creatures. Where he may safely operate is in the region of a character's free will, in the perfecting of a character's free decisions and behavior. Still further, Luzán finds it necessary to specify that the poet cannot perfect the objects of God's natural world which must be represented as in fact they actually are, "because the Author of nature has made them as they ought to be." [31] But the poet may beautify them—sprinkling meadows with flowers, for example—without departing from nature as he has found it.

To us such distinctions seem artificial. But Luzán belonged to an exactingly theological milieu. The slightest suggestion that a poet could perfect the work already perfected by the Creator would produce, and not in Spain only, an overwhelming flood of censure. Luzán was too orthodox by conviction to make any such suggestion. But in all other ways, his understanding of the universal as an imitation of what "ought to be," or "what could be," became so intricately involved in the understanding of verisimilitude that attention was diverted from the former to the latter. Luzán closes the important Chapter IX with a thought from Horace, though he does not mention Horace's name, to the effect that in both particular and universal imitation the poet must represent nature by means of "verisimilitude" and make the hero "in a certain episode, agitated by a certain passion, behave and speak as is natural to his temperament and habits." [32]

If this is a pitiful travesty of what a genius intuitively would understand by a convincing imitation of the universal and the particular, it is at any rate as near as any modern Preceptist had got to the difficult mind of Aristotle.

V *The Purpose of Poetry*

Having discussed the essence of poetry and the imitative means by which poetry functions, Luzán, in his last chapter of Book I, comes logically to determine why poetry should be written at all. It is only, of course, in more modern times that the justification for any of the arts could be thought to consist merely in the artist's compulsive desire to express himself. Formerly it was generally assumed that poetry must have some philosophical purpose, some logical place in a logical universe where all things work together for an obvious general good. Plato, first, trying to fit the artist into his ideal Republic, and later, aesthetic welfare workers and Christian guardians of public morals had related arts to public benefits. Aristotle's idea of the purpose of art was much more liberal and allowed for the maturing experience of the enjoyment of beauty for its own sake. Which idea, simplified by

Horace, passed into the Neoclassical codebook as a poetic effect called "pleasure."

This chapter, therefore, balances various modern sets of views on the subject against each other. Is the purpose of poetry chiefly one of utility? Is it pleasure? Or, could poetry possibly have more than one purpose, as Horace and Muratori suggest? By now we know Luzán well enough to guess that, given three possibilities, here utility, pleasure, or both, he is likely to choose the least dogmatic. Already in this book he has sensibly declared that healthy enjoyment is a form of utility. We then expect him to find that the purpose of poetry is neither simple nor single, but broad and complex. And this, after giving what he considers to be proper value to his reader by reasoning on all the various possibilities, is in fact the conclusion he eventually reaches.

It must be admitted, however, that since the inner nature of poetry has not been adequately defined either in Luzán's *Poetics* or in any other Neoclassical treatise, he repeats himself a good deal without seriously furthering his philosophical point. The difference between pleasure and utility becomes more artificial than in his eager seriousness he means it to be. Nevertheless, he comes well out of this international debate by comparing his authorities objectively. With all due respect to Beni, he declares, moving, as is his custom, towards the most solid ground visible, he, Don Ignacio, cannot see why the poet in this respect should differ from, for instance, the architect, who does not design always for the same purpose, but sometimes designs recreational buildings, and at other times purely utilitarian ones. The poet, then, may surely write sometimes for one, sometimes for the other, sometimes for both purposes, is his final verdict. Luzán's reasoning and conclusion may be inadequate, though he is less superficial than most Neoclassicists. But at least his method of arguing leaves room for adjustments in later books, allows for reasonableness, and protects the new century's growing need for mental maneuverability.

CHAPTER 8

The Poetics. *Book II.*
Consideration of the Lyric

IN his introductory book Luzán had philosophically asked and rationally answered a number of general questions. What is poetry? How did it come into being? What forms did it take? What is its present condition? How should it continue to develop? What should be the poet's ultimate aim? . . . Book II, entitled "On Poetic Utility and Delight," in part pursues the same discussion. But incidentally it resolves itself into the first of three specific and practical inquiries, divided into Books II, III, and IV on the history, nature, and development of lyrical, dramatic, and epic poetry respectively. Therefore, although Book II deals broadly with the justification of poetry and poets, and continues to discuss, especially in early chapters, those large aesthetic questions like "What is poetic utility, delight, beauty, truth?" Luzán's illustrations of the service rendered by poetry to the cause of beauty, etc., are largely taken from the Lyric, and eventually Book II settles down practically to analyze all the component parts of lyrical verse. In the 1737 edition, these illustrations chiefly reflect Luzán's familiarity with Classical Ancients and Classically-inspired moderns, including Spanish Renaissance writers from the fifteenth century onwards. But in the 1789 version, Spanish national poets of the Middle and Golden Ages crowd, one might almost say, stampede the text in such a rush of self-assertiveness as to suggest that Luzán and Llaguno had become overwhelmed by the major discovery of Peninsular prolificity, and were still engaged in trying, against odds, to marshal the swarming poets and poems into significant order.

Logical and practical though Luzán's arrangement is in 1737, it involves some repetition out of very thoroughness. In all three books he is anxious to demonstrate how each of the genres concerned can be justified on grounds of utility and delight, and how each in its peculiar way imitates life in fact or in fictitious probability. To a certain degree, every book is roughly self-contained, and Luzán's philosophical principles could be understood from any one of them in isolation. In order, therefore, to avoid unnecessary repetition of his basic ideas in the three books, we shall ignore his reassertions of the same principles except where they are given some new significance or emphasis.

I *Preoccupation with Poetic Duty*

The first chapter of Book II, the whole of which book reasons obsessively about the principle of utility in poetic expression and passes on the argument to its two successors, is a typical eighteenth-century statement of the ethics of artistic enjoyment. Pedagogic to a degree, the Age of Reason placed the poet's responsibility for edifying the public in the forefront of their privileges and obligations alike. So that Don Ignacio's own natural procedure was to cultivate his aesthetic territory as an area which, while not swamped by Moral Philosophy, was to be lavishly watered by its requirements. The first law of poetry, he might well have said in so many words, is the moral law. For, despite his concessions to the utility of wholesome pleasure, it is the solid, wholesome qualification and not the trumperiness of pleasure for pleasure's sake which bears his calculated stress. Consequently his conspicuous opening chapter, "On the Meaning and Origin of Poetic Utility," starts, as his most serious arguments always start, with a philosophical review of moral principles. His voice, soberly pitched to match the occasion, might suggest that he is engaged on a religious commentary—on St. Augustine or St. Thomas Aquinas, for example. Man, runs the standard Christian apology he employs, man, in his original state of innocence, needed no guide from Arts or Science to achieve and enjoy eternal felicity. On the other hand, fallen man, dependent on exterior aids, yet in his weakness unable to withstand the full force of stark morality, finds unadorned philosophy too erudite and impracticable a discipline to take advantage of its help. It is all very well, adds Don Ignacio, for the philosopher to assert that a poor man can be virtuously happy if he wants to be, or that it is a finer thing to conquer a passion than to conquer another man's person. True though such thoughts ideally may be, pure philosophy is too bleak for the average mind, and starkness and severity alone are unlikely to convince the majority of poor, passionate men. This, accordingly, is where the Arts assume the task, which philosophy cannot undertake, of persuading by an appeal to the heart rather than to the head.

If this apology now seems inadequate or unnecessary, it was well calculated in its time to anticipate puritanical criticism. Aristotle too, not to mention his modern disciples, held the belief that all forms of poetry should in some way be philosophically justifiable, though the modern apologist was the more committed to specific causes. For his part, as if to stamp his aesthetic conclusions with the impress of Christian sanctity, Luzán approves the pleasurable persuasiveness of poetry by saying that it infiltrates surreptitiously into the "interior castle" [1] of the heart where, by strategy, it achieves what knowledge achieves only by war. Probably Luzán did not know, or remember, that his image of the "interior castle" had been sanctified mystically by Santa Teresa de Jesús. But he was aware, his reverent tone suggests, that he was treading holy ground, and the claims of poetry seem to acquire thereby some reflected beatitude.

Thus elaborately, thus, as he would see it, rationally, Luzán proceeds towards the establishment of poetry in all its disguises as a potentially useful agent of moral reform. It is true that Epic and Drama to him, as to other Neoclassicists, were more obvious means of improving public morals than the Lyric, especially the Lyric at its most flimsy, flitting, and elusive. Nevertheless, a moral case is duly made out for the Lyric as a preliminary to the detailed treatment which this form of verse is to receive later. If Luzán sounds a little grudging in his conclusion that lyrical poetry is only "fairly useful and profitable," [2] this is not because, as we know from his own poetry, he himself despises lighter moods and meters. It is rather that he has difficulty in rationalizing their moral significance. Possibly he thought of lyrical poetry as the mere pastime it was for himself: though a pastime legitimate so long as it was inoffensive. "Thank God," he said, that licentious subjects, "contrary to modesty and propriety," were not, so far as he knew, to be found in Spanish poets.[3] Perhaps it was well for his peace of mind that his knowledge, even by 1754, did not in this respect go any farther, did not, for instance, go back to the fourteenth century to the earthy Juan Ruiz.

Being hard pressed, so he must have imagined, to prove a large usefulness for the Lyric, Luzán concentrates on the features most self-evidently didactic. As listed by any Neoclassical theorist, these usually sound as chilling as the stark philosophy which they are supposed persuasively to represent as aids to fallen mankind. Luzán's list is drawn up in the same tradition. To be told that the utility of lyrical poetry lies in satire, in its praise of virtue, in moral reflections, in serious, improving love poems that eschew sensuality and express shame for past error, is indeed to be given an impression of something forbiddingly unsonglike. Moreover in Chapter III, "On the Instruction Provided by All Arts and Sciences," Don Ignacio, overlooking no recognized principle of guidance, gives explicit directions on how the poet is to furnish his instruction: by outright maxims, he says, or grave teaching of a moral nature; by informative discourses on, for instance, military techniques; by his geographical and historical detail; by reflections on the ways of the world, especially on the hypocrisy of men-about-court; and, significantly for this usually polite and discreet academician, on that monster they call "Reason of State."[4] Had Luzán not added some equally serious injunctions on the exercise of moderation in all things, had he not insisted more than once that success depends on knowing just where to insert instruction and how to disguise it, the ideal lyrical poetry he was describing might have sounded too good to be bearable.

Yet, in all fairness to Luzán, poetry lovers of any century must know exactly what he meant, most of all when he instanced model lyricists like Horace, Boscán, and Garcilaso. Perhaps a more attractive way of explaining himself would have been not merely to quote from great and thoughtful poets, but to analyze inspiring passages, examining minutely their verbal and philosophical content, and relating them to the poet's personality which holds words and thoughts together and gives them individual suggestiveness. Let us remember, however, that analytical methods in the modern sense were hardly known in eighteenth-century literary criticism. The hallowed technique was to proceed not from practice to theory, but vice versa, and, until the literary critic learned to imitate the scientific practitioner, his theories would always sound inadequate. Usually, not being much of a poet himself, he failed to account for the arresting effect produced by a poet's philosophical reflection at the right psychological moment of the poem. Luzán would have approved Wordsworth's experience of being "disturbed" by the "joy of elevated thought," [5] when the loveliness of woods and fields enabled this Englishman, as he sensitively built up the sublimity of their appeal, to raise his thought to the supramaterial level of all ultimate values. Luzán would have appreciated the thoughtfulness of Luis de León's "Tranquil Night" with its receptive word "contemplate" in the first line, "When I contemplate the heavens," [6] without realizing, probably, that so much of the effect depends on León's air of receptivity, and that the word "contemplate" of the first line is made, from its strategically unobtrusive position, to represent volumes of unspoken longings towards the infinite.

The earnestness of Luzán's convictions about the joy of elevated thought in poetry is demonstrated at this point by insertions in the 1789 version, where additional stress is placed on the desirability of cultivating sublimer poetic thinking. Taken out of its eighteenth-century context, his impatience with sensory love themes and madrigal casualness looks like the churlishness of a spoilsport, single-minded dominie. Who else could resist the blackbird notes of love madrigals of the Golden Age? But the plain fact of the eighteenth century was that love poetry had become a sterile exercise in trite gallantries, and that love themes, perhaps like modern sex themes, had been mercilessly overplayed. Therefore we should not be misled by Luzán's impatience with love poetry. He expressed a deep eighteenth-century need for change of poetic direction. Indeed by Luzán's time, eighteenth-century poetry had been neither edifying nor artistic, but had deteriorated into insensate repetition.

II   *Poetry for Pleasure. The Nature and Function of Beauty*

Once his thoughts on the moral and philosophical responsibilities of poetry are unequivocally established as basic principles, Luzán is free to examine qualities which make poetry, and now the Lyric especially, a source of pleasure. This examination constitutes the main body of Book II, some of which shows Luzán at his best and some at his worst. It would seem that Don Ignacio rises to an occasion most successfully when he can exercise his empiric common sense. His general remarks about, and his detailed examination of poetic realism and verisimilitude, for instance, are almost invariably arresting, and, though not original, had been personally thought out and assessed by him. Chapters in Book II on these matters are among the most interesting of all of his output. Subjects of a more abstract nature—the meaning of poetic *beauty* or *tenderness,* for example—seem to send him more dependently to his authorities. Book II, then, serves admirably to show him in his weakness and his strength.

One cause of weakness, not only in Luzán but in all Neoclassicists is the preconditioning technique they inherited from formal philosophy. Neoclassicists, Luzán foremost among them, recognized the need for a revolution in subject matter. They were less aware, though awareness would come with time, that their commitments with old techniques of criticism prevented them from fully understanding shapes of thought and expression to which they were unaccustomed. They were not yet ready for the technical repercussions of the scientific revolution.

A clear example of this weakness is revealed in Chapter IV, "Concerning Poetic Delight and the Two Principles on which Delight Is Based, Beauty and Tenderness." Because it was customary to proceed from theoretic principle to poetic practice, Luzán is committed at the outset to the artificial activity of distinguishing between "Beauty" and "Tenderness"—his word for the latter is *dulzura,* literally *sweetness*—separately and together, whereas the truly empiric, the scientific method would have been to analyze individual passages, postponing any deduction about relationships between Beauty and Tenderness until other findings were complete. By tradition Luzán feels obliged to regard Beauty and Tenderness as essentially separate entities, to grade them preferentially, and to see Tenderness as an enhancement and addition to Beauty rather than one of the many qualities or forms of Beauty. Traditional methods of organizing thought induced coherence, yet for practical purposes they were liable to discourage analytical reasoning in all but the most original thinkers.

In the present instance, Luzán's immediate authority, Muratori, had neatly standardized a poetic ideal requiring the combination of Goodness and Beauty and an alliance of the two with Truth, the source, he explained, of poetic Utility and Delight.[7] So that Beauty became the Light which adorns Truth. Guided by this Philosophical management, Luzán was able competently to organize his own major chapters of Book II: "Concerning Delight," "Beauty," "Truth." Further, Horace had asserted that it was not enough for poetry to be beautiful *(pulchra)*, it must also be attractive, or pleasing; and the Latin *dulcia*, looking so similar to Italian *dolce* and Spanish *dulce*, had been misinterpreted as "sweet," or "tender" and produced the artificial distinction, "It is not enough for poetry to be beautiful, it must also be tender (or sweet)" on which some of Don Ignacio's poorest reasoning is based.[8] So bemused, in fact, is he with these philosophical distinctions, themselves not very deeply philosophical, that although he is ready enough to give examples of Tenderness, he misses the more important opportunity for exemplifying Beauty without Tenderness and so leaves us with only a vague idea of what the distinction really meant to him if, indeed, he was completely clear about it himself. We know that the Aragonese did not invariably follow his authorities blindly. But on this minor question, as he may have thought of it, Horace's words, or what he took to be Horace's words, had automatically set up in his mind a plan of detailed exposition which prevented him from appreciating Horace's true meaning. Luzán even seems satisfied with a distinction making Beauty intellectual in its effects and Tenderness emotive. Beauty, he says far too categorically, pleases the understanding and Tenderness "always delights and always moves the affections."[9] More, he goes to the bookish, the "owlish" as his colleague José Villarroel from the Academy of Good Taste would have thought, extreme of indicating that though Beauty—that is, in its dazzlingly intellectual capacity—might detract from the immediate force of truth, Tenderness is incapable of any such deception. The Preceptist was incautiously treading extremely dangerous ground.

The Spanish word *"dulzura"* which we have translated as *tenderness*, appeared to suggest to Luzán a human capacity for sympathy with fellow suffering, and one of his poorest chapters, Chapter V, "On Poetic Tenderness," is based on the artificial assumption that *dulzura* is an aspect of nature, and therefore is self-evident and constant, apparently in the sense that a natural person is normally affected by the sight of another man's pain, and that nature, of which Tenderness is an aspect, normally observes consistent laws and patterns. Beauty—generally equated by Luzán with technical excellence—may be, he adds, inconstant. It did not occur to the Preceptist, who was thinking his way through formal classification, that what might seem tender to one critic might seem insipid to another, and that repeated sensibility can become nauseatingly cloying as the eighteenth-century sentimental plays and sentimental novels were soon to prove.

It is true that Luzán's conception of poetic Tenderness at its best is the disciplined Renaissance conception: a moderate, controlled expression of feeling exteriorized, in Classical, eclogue-like simplicity, in highly selective circumstances and with philosophical overtones. But, even so, his artificial separation of Tenderness and Beauty leads him into absurd arguments. He can be heard asserting that too much beauty sometimes diminishes a total (literary) effect. As if too much sensibility would not destroy it altogether! Garcilaso, he says, when amplifying one of Martial's themes with feelings of his own, chose to make the poem less beautiful in order to make it more tender. One tender sonnet of Garcilaso, he argues in the same context, is worth more than all the affectation of Góngora. As if the two technically different styles could reasonably be compared. As if the poet's poet, Garcilaso, represented a tenderness which made beauty beautiful, whereas the critic's favorite target, Góngora, represented beauty in isolation, in its intrinsic inadequacy. The argument is particularly ill-conceived because Luzán did not believe that Góngora's obscurity could constitute beauty at all.

Still, once Luzán begins explicity to dictate rules for the production of Tenderness as the crowning glory of Beauty (Chapter VI), he becomes more convincing. We may not nowadays be able to share his belief that a knowledge of formal Rhetoric will further a poet's practice in this art. Nor are we nowadays greatly impressed by the technical means he instances for moving the affections, least of all the use of exclamation and apostrophe. It was because Neoclassicists were so observant of the letter of the law of Rhetoric that they produced such excruciatingly comic tragedies as Nicolás Fernández de Moratín's *Hormesinda*. Which was a pity. For several midcentury tragedians, Montiano and Cadalso for example, were able dramatists, and many lyrical poets, Luzán included, improved in proportion as they dispensed with academic self-consciousness.

But Luzán, prompted by Quintilian, does not forget to prescribe the most practical rule of all: that a poet should "identify himself with the affections he imitates (from life)." [10] Also the examples he gives from favorite poets in their quiet moods of sensibility:

Sappho, Virgil, Horace, Garcilaso, and, in the second thoughts of 1789, Luis de León, prove his good taste and show that while his intellectual argument is poor, his artistic judgment is sound.

One of the main reasons why Luzán sees poetic Tenderness as a vital addition to Beauty rather than a particular mood or aspect of it, dependent on the poet's own mood and purpose, is his acceptance of Muratori's argument that Beauty is the light of Truth, by which is also understood Moral Truth. Academically defined, or rather explained away thus, for this is no real definition or explanation, Beauty certainly assumes a stark abstractness, a white perfection of virtuosity, which understandably leaves Luzán very coldly disposed towards it. His earnest attempts to promote the interests of Tenderness are attempts to put color into Beauty's cheeks. The idea that Beauty is the light of Truth meant genuinely to him that obscurity of expression, the splendid obscurity, for instance, of the Spanish Góngora, could not by definition be beautiful. Again traditional syllogism obstructed critical freedom. Beauty is light. Obscurity is not light. Therefore obscurity cannot possibly be beautiful.[11]

III   *What is Poetic Truth?*

Luzán's examination of Truth, understood by him to be that basic reality which Beauty illuminated and Tenderness made acceptable, brings us to two of the scholar's best chapters in Book II: Chapters VIII and IX. These, to a certain extent, offset his previous vagueness both about Light and Truth, even if they fail to clarify the meaning of Beauty itself.

As before, he resorts to classification. But now he is drawing also on his own reading experience, is shaking his thought free from the predisposing terminology of the Schools, and is able to develop his argument with a certain personal vitality. Chapter VIII, "On the Two Kinds of Truth, Actual and Probable," influenced by Muratori on the same theme, is concerned largely with the basic distinction between actual Truth, as sought by historians and scientists, and Truth as envisaged by poets. Among facts of actual truth, we must understand, were still classed the truths of theological dogma. Theology continued to be regarded as scientifically proved fact. To the mind of the first half of the Age of Reason, in most parts of Europe, truth could not be accepted as truth on empiric evidence unless it could also be proved by theoretic reasoning. The twentieth century demands a different act of theological faith. It assumes that we may rightly believe in something which cannot scientifically be proved. This distinction is an important factor in our understanding of earlier epochs. An eighteenth-century believer was more alarmed or outraged by threats to his Faith than is the modern believer, because he could still think definitive proof to be possible. He continued to think that one system of universal ideology which logically accounted for God and man, and the relationship between them, must be wholly and in every part complete forever. The twentieth century realizes that nothing has ever, scientifically or otherwise, been completely explained and is more used both to disbelief and to acts of faith in face of open doubt. Among Luzán's examples of proved, incontrovertible fact—that the earth is round, that certain events have historically happened—he includes what to him is the scientific fact that God exists and is eternal.

The other kind of Truth, Probability or Poetic Truth, is lucidly explained in the following chapter as whatever, in real or imagined circumstances, is acceptable or believable. We should now say what, in any circumstances, seems to the observer plausible. Myths, allegories, and strange figures of speech which, directly or indirectly, express credible concepts, ideas true absolutely or hypothetically—all such aspects of fact and imagination are included in this category. Luzán's argument is that the existence of poetic Beauty must depend on one of these two forms of Truth; that Poetic Beauty must illuminate either what the reader or hearer knows to be true, or what he can believe as likely. In this sense the Neoclassicists' conception of Truth as something proved by reason becomes much more understandable. Broadly their idea of obscurity, darkly concealing reality, is accordingly of something which cannot be accepted because it seems a negation of understanding and cannot be believed as likely. It is in the prejudices of their applications, their contempt for Góngora, for example, rather than in their general reasoning, that the modern critic would differ from them.

The 1789 edition adds an observation very typical of Luzán. Though he had made generous room for imagination, he was too Classically disposed to enjoy imagination in profusion—which certainly in lesser poets, of whom probably he was not especially thinking, is objectionable—and he appended reproving notes on metaphorical exaggeration, or the Untrue (Chapter VIII). Insofar as he was thinking of the use of exaggerated metaphors for their own sake, the note does not come amiss. Even nonsense verse obeys the laws of likelihood within a given topsy-turviness. Metaphors of relationships that "lie" are generally metaphors which are devoid of acceptable meaning.

When making distinctions about Truth, which, outside the preserves of Christian dogma, Luzán regarded fairly empirically, he does not betray the same fundamental weakness as he betrayed in his chapters on Beauty. There he had expounded the nature of Beauty when enhanced by Tenderness, while failing to characterize Beauty when Tenderness was absent. But in Chapter IX, "On Verisimilitude,"—that is, Poetic Truth based on Aristotle's reasoning about probability, he fairly examines his subject from all sides and explains satisfactorily both what is plausible and what is not.

Those medieval tales or poems of magic, the chivalresque stories with their dragons, spells, and abnormal feats of arms in ungeographical places, were not meant, Luzán knows, as allegories or symbols. To many people, he therefore concludes, they must have seemed implausible, the implication being that in certain other sections of the community they were accepted. This brings him into agreement with Muratori who had explained that verisimilitude can be of two degrees: popular, and, in Luzán's own phrase, "noble," that is, cultured or educated. There are, Don Ignacio further reflects, with due caution, some sophisticated examples of improbabilities, like Ariosto's *Orlando furioso* whose appeal may be ascribed to the attractiveness of artifice and ingenuity.

Thus far modern critics can easily follow. Possibly they would only disagree with *Luzán* over his assumption that "popular" verisimilitude must be artistically inferior to "noble." At the same time, it would take little extension of Luzán's own argument to cover the licensing of any truly imaginative fairy tale. Verisimilitude by his own account means that which can be accepted. And spells and marvels can only be accepted if the author has either the ability to charm a reader sufficiently to make him feel happy and acclimatized in strange settings, or has the wit so to mix fiction with circumstantial fact that strangeness seems logical, as it does in the half-truths of modern science fiction.

Evidently thoughts of a not dissimilar nature had duly occurred to Luzán. And the most likable feature of this lively chapter is a personal doubt which he expounds refreshingly. In general, it rises from the impatience shared by practical thinkers of the Enlightenment with verbal sophistry, and with technically elaborate ways of saying something self-evidently simple. Could there be a case, Don Ignacio now wonders, in his determination to explore all the possibilities of a subject patently fascinating to him, could there be a case in which "verisimilitude" passes the limits of the possible? "I mean is only the possible verisimilar, or could impossible things sometimes be verisimilar and so some truth be exemplified which is inverisimilar and incredible?" [12]

At first it would seem, thinks Luzán, that such a strange case might be defended. But it is when he refers to aesthetic authorities on the subject: G. C. Orsi, F. Bonamici, and L. Castelvetro, that his impatience with dialectical niceties breaks into constructive activity. In support of the reality of untrue verisimilitude and inverisimilar truth, Bonamici had asserted that what is true and possible may occasionally diverge from what is credible, because the credible and possible are the results of different operations of understanding. Castelvetro had then tortuously explained possibility as "that potentiality in an action which finds no impossibility in the realization of such an action," [13] and credibility as the assumption that an action may be realized. Further, that nature and opinion have different confines. So that one thing can be possible but not credible, another credible but not possible; and that if the possible may pass beyond the credible, the credible at times may exceed what seems to be possible.

This hairsplitting is too much for Luzán's practical common sense. He bluntly objects to the obscurity of the whole argument which looks, he says disparagingly, very like mere sophistry. Taking, therefore, a deep breath of fresh air, he treats the distinctions to a few tonic comments. If the Bonamici-Castelvetro argument merely means that men are frequently deceived in their judgments, that fact is too obvious to warrant discussion. But if their argument poses the paradox that truth, recognized as such, can be improbable, and if the impossible, recognized as such, can be credible, then their argument must surely be untenable.

Because, goes on Luzán briskly, nature is one thing and our opinion of it another. It is not strange that our opinion of what nature is should fail to conform with the reality, not strange that something should be impossible in itself, yet possible in our opinion, and vice versa. What cannot be accepted is the suggestion that our opinion can hold something to be true and at the same time hold it to be false.

On this point, as we have seen, Luzán might not convince later critics who can believe that readers may disbelieve intellectually and believe imaginatively in the same thing at the same time. But a modern critic would sympathize with Luzán's impatience at the finicky terminology of the Bonamici-Castelvetro contortions. Particularly he would sympathize with Luzán's objection to the idea that possibility is "that potentiality which finds no impossibility in realizing itself" and would enjoy Luzán's treatment of the pretentiousness of the pair and his contention that their use of the words *possible* and *impossible* have only succeeded in making obscurity more obscure than ever:

". . . because if the term possibility is obscure, so is the term impossible also: which means that one obscure thing is being defined by another equally obscure thing, and that shadows are being piled on shadows. Altogether this definition to my way of thinking means that the *possible is something which is not impossible* and the other definition may likewise be summarized in the words *that the credible is something which can be believed.* But all that is already known by anybody and does not need a definition to explain it." [14]

Here was a scholar, robustly alive, whom it must have been a pleasure to meet.

IV *Literary Qualities*

Once the large, abstract question about Beauty and Truth is, for his own purposes, satisfactorily answered, and the ethical principles of poetry recorded, Luzán is free to examine the purely literary qualities of poetic expression and to face that most formidable fact of Baroque power, the mesmerizing cult of the metaphor. Throughout the remainder of this book, therefore, he is less concerned with poets' obligations and public commitments and more with their artistry. For the same reason his attention shifts from poetic potentiality to poetic achievement.

[120]

Significantly, his first literary concern is with subject matter, and very rightly so. No advance on tedious mediocrity could be made in mideighteenth-century Spain until artists found new sources of material. Everything, it seemed, that could be said on traditional poetic themes had been said already. The old sentiments had been wrung dry. The old thoughts had been rendered meaningless by repetition. Consequently Luzán's insistence here, as in various other places, on the poets' need to think, to seek new "marvels"—verisimilar marvels, needless to say —his encouragement to poets discreetly to exercise their imaginations for themselves, meant that he had recognized the practical need for new poets to come to terms with their own times.[15] A poet will find fresh material, he says, comparing notes with Muratori, by qualities of soul: by inventiveness combined with imagination, and controlled by Judgment, their head.

Don Ignacio himself would later lead the way—not very brilliantly perhaps, but suggestively—in the ideology of his poem, *The Judgment of Paris.*[16] The new ideas of any period are seldom used most effectively by authors who first introduced them. Usually new ideas are expressed with more originality after they have been assimilated and applied to individual or social experience. Enthusiasm, coupled with unease over scientific change and social uncertainty, would eventually inspire later poets to more original utterance. In the meantime Luzán's constant reference to that urgent need for new ideas, and his imaginative exercise of new ideas have a value which could hardly be overstressed. Let us say to our own times, is the burden of his message, something worth saying, and let us say it in such a way that posterity will think it worthy of preservation. But the crux of the problem is in the "newness" of the material. Can instructions be given for the discovery of something new? We expect Luzán to be at a loss. But he is not. New material is to be found, he goes on penetratingly, by searching in a proposed subject for the truths least known about that subject, the truths which have been least observed, and then presenting them with telling comparison, opportune repetition, and imaginative use of the various technical subtleties of style and diction.[17] The suggestion is thoroughly realistic.

Although Luzán just now is closely following in Muratori's footstep, he displays his aptitude for exemplifying what he approves in his authorities by means of his own independent observation. Here he turns to the very modern exponents of new rationalism, John Locke and *The Spectator*. Presumably he had read neither in English. His reference to *The Spectator* is by its French subtitle, *The Modern Socrates*.[18] But both English authorities are summoned in Chapter XII which deals with fresh means of presenting desirably original ideas and modern points of view. Locke's philosophy of sensuality which Luzán does not completely approve, is at least acceptable to him in that it illustrates how knowledge of objects comes to us through the senses and imprints images on the understanding; also, by extension, how imagery is derived and operates in literature. *The Spectator*, itself influenced by Locke, is called upon to elaborate the same idea by classifying images received from the understanding into two groups, primitive and derived: that is, direct description and metaphorical; the splendid directness of Homeric description, the combination of nature and artifice in Virgil, says Luzán, or the metaphorical, the "enchanted country" of Ovid's *Metamorphoses*.[19]

Not only did Luzán turn for confirmation, in so far as was discreet, to some of the Rationalists who were conditioning the century's mind in preparation for the new Physicists. He had the independence to choose his literary illustrations for himself. His Spanish examples from Renaissance writers onwards are suitably numerous. Nor was he so prejudiced against Golden Age playwrights that he could not quote or refer to some of their unforgettable lines or praise their verbal inventiveness. When he instances successful writers of imaginative description, his list includes Calderón, Lupercio de Argensola, "Tomé de Burguillos" (Lope de Vega), Ulloa, and other Spaniards. Furthermore, he is willing to admit that the Ancients themselves had their unfortunate moments. When encouraging poets to practice word painting with a subtle interplay of the explicit and the suggestive, and when warning them not to abuse their descriptive art by overelaborateness, he illustrates his warning not only with lines from Golden Age dramatists who had sinned, he thought, but from the Peninsular Classicists' distinguished ancestor, Seneca, who makes the King of Thebes in *Oedipus* flowerily declaim, to the detriment of dramatic urgency.

Evidently Luzán, dallying in the pleasure grounds of metaphor, liked to linger relaxedly over the use and interpretation of figurative speech. Metaphors produced some of the "wonders" of his poetic estate. They engineered those personifications of nature in his "enchanted world" where everything has "body, soul, and sense, where plants love and beasts complain . . . and woods have ears . . ." [20] In a section roughly covering Chapters XIII-XV, where he still keeps close to Muratori, his commentary is quickened by dedicated enthusiasm and personal understanding. The peaks of his argument rise with gratifying conspicuousness above the general level of his procedure: a feature of academic landscape which could not be taken for granted in the early eighteenth century. For instance, after classifying metaphors, as his authorities had taught him, into natural and artificial—the first obviously direct and simple descriptions of nature like Argensola's *Lleva tras sí los pámpanos octubre* ("October carries off the tender vines") [21] the second, at an artificial remove from reality like "the hill supports the heavens"—he rises from definition and example to proclaim that the essential value of the metaphor is to oblige the understanding to learn a new truth, or to see an old truth from a new angle. There is a significant difference, he explains, between an unfigurative description of the sun shining on a meadow and the metaphorical phrase "smiling meadow." If the meadow "smiles" it has personified responsiveness, and is like a man, thinks Luzán, entering creatively into the situation, who responds to the laughter of a companion.[22] It is an attractive point.

With regard to the figure of the sky upheld by the column, as it were, of the mountain, Luzán observes appreciatively that the poet passing from one natural metaphor—the mountain seeming to touch the sky—which might felicitously occur to anyone, has fabricated for himself a complex image entirely of his own imagination: an image, we might say, within an image. The Preceptist now is not just dictating. He is engaged in genuine analysis, and thinking aloud, it appears, as he goes along. If the mountain, he reflects, seems to us to touch the sky, it therefore may be imagined to act as a supporting column. That image of touching may indeed suggest itself to us all when we look at the natural phenomenon. But the column, Luzán marvels, is a suggestive parallel provided by the poet who implies, without explaining, the comparison he has in mind.

"Wonders" like these, giving creative life to what is ordinary in nature or provoking entirely new trends of thought and exquisitely new refinements of sentiment in human circumstances, go far to explain to Luzán's practical mind those flights of genius which he delightedly calls *arrobos,* a soaring ecstasy in which "the masters fly so high that they are almost lost to sight." [23] The idea was not his own. He was glossing Muratori who had spoken of flights of genius, and of poetic *furore.* But Luzán could imaginatively act on a hint and, of the two, his own description is the more excited, as if he were personally and appreciatively entering into the spirit of poetic flights. "They are so moved and their imagination is so greatly inflamed with excitement that, carried out of themselves, they look like different people and talk in a different way. Then, following on the swift flight of their stirring imagination, they reach the heavens, move over the past and the future, enter, as it were, into another world, and everything they see and say is strange, is splendid, is wonderful." [24]

If this is not an analysis of genius, at least it is an inspiring explanation of the effect of genius, and for a moment transforms the dry scholar Luzán into a personality as responsive as his companionably smiling meadow.

His absorbing study of the metaphor, however, leads Luzán to conclusions with which a present-day critic could not fully agree. He would approve Don Ignacio's dislike of metaphors that are overdone or inartistically used as a parade of showy ingenuity, and would appreciate his general advice on proportion and discriminate good taste, the infused or acquired sense of balance which prevents good poets from falling from their dizzy heights. He would be pleased to hear the Preceptist defending vivid images—like that of the mountains holding up the sky—as seeming false only to men of overliteral understanding and justifiably true, or verisimilous, to men of imagination. Naturally, however, Luzán could not accept the figurative dislocations or transpositions with which, at their best, the Baroque descriptive writers projected themselves spiritually into the twentieth century. To paint a horse with a human head, Horace had objected, was to paint a ridiculous monstrosity. Consequently, to describe one sense impression in terms of another—like, let us say *blue notes*— or apply to the abstract a qualification normally applied to the concrete—like *blue falsehood*—was, Neoclassically speaking, to indulge in anti-artistic absurdities.

Judging by Neoclassical principles, then, Luzán could be

guaranteed to find that the imagery, even of the best Baroque exponents, Italian or Spanish, was grotesquely distorted, and he could not be expected to see that distortions might be as intellectually and imaginatively acceptable in literature as are the distortions of El Greco in paint. Calderón provides him with what he considers a suitable parallel to Horace's monstrous horse. The Baroque dramatist had described the translation into heaven of certain persons as the "blue falsehood" of peoples. Luzán could not follow the imaginative logic of intellectually transposing the blue of the sky to qualify an impression of miracle-bafflement, and he pedantically explains that the component parts of an image must have an exact interrelationship of figure, action, and effect. The phrase "an arrow flies," he says, shows a true parallel between the flight of an arrow and the flight of a bird. But "blue falsehood" provides no parallel of like with like. Similarly he rejects Góngora's "I shall weave your memory among the peoples," and his more obscure "that shadows seal in sepulchres of foam," [25] a reference to black print on white paper, as images fit for nothing but derision. To Luzán, in fact, the Baroque world was permanently barred. It is not necessary to add that Chapter XV, in which these examples occur, develops in part into a Neoclassical attack on Spain's most extreme form of the Baroque, Gongorism.

One of his most revealing denunciations, however, concerns an engaging line in Sonnet 43, by the no means extreme Lope de Vega: "And where you are not with me, there is no day." [26] Here even a Neoclassicist, one might have thought, could have justified the exaggeration as the verisimilar impression made on the speaker's imagination by his distracted anguish. But it appears that in Luzán's example is involved another sacred Neoclassical principle: one that we must understand to be essential if we are to enter any Neoclassicist's mind. The line assumes a false syllogism which meant more, we must try to realize, to the Neoclassicist than the image itself. Figures of speech had little value for him in themselves. He thought of them as explicit messengers of a logical masterthought. Nowadays we may string a line of images across a poem, or a line of adjectives or nouns, without a single word of reasoning, and call it poetry. For poetry to us may be legitimately concerned with one unrelated impression alone, or with the significant atmospheric force of a series of unrelated impressions. In this instance Lope offends Luzán primarily by what the latter calls false reasoning, by the use, he protests, of exaggerated paradoxes, and a lazy readiness to pander to the superficially minded general public with cheap contrivances to catch attention. In all seriousness Luzán explains the sin against Rhetoric in this sonnet. First the poet, he reflects, exaggerates the violence of his passion by referring to his lady as the sun. On top of this extravagance he then creates a false argument, trying seriously to show that, although the real sun may go down, night does not fall, because his metaphorical sun is still present. Even worse, pursues Luzán, is a lover's logic in a different sonnet, 94, on a similar subject where poetic reasoning wrongly proves that the lady, while physically far away is not, on that account, absent because a sunrise is seen from every direction and so the sun-lady is always visible somewhere: a false conception, Luzán objects, which only the ignorant could accept. For anyone who troubles to analyze the sentiment will soon discover that, in order to break down the whole concept, it is merely necessary to observe that the metaphorical sun of a lady is not the same as a true sun and has not the same attributes.

Here no doubt Luzán's "owlishness" would have been as amusing to Lope as Lope's reasoning was to Luzán who would permit such "exaggerations" to jocular verse only. In this case, too, the Preceptist displays the greatest weakness of the purist Neoclassicist, or indeed professed Preceptists of any aesthetic faith. They could not allow for the unforeseen qualities of genius, for chance, or for any aesthetic orientation not their own. On this occasion Luzán could not countenance an artistic logic different from the logic of formal philosophy which implied at least tacit syllogism. However Luzán, to his own satisfaction, did find a way around imaginative difficulties of the kind. If only poets would use modifying phrases like *it seems, one would say, one would think* . . . much of the difficulty might be avoided, he thought. For support over this recommendation he incautiously turns to "a most lovely image" employed by the "most learned Feijoo." "Incautiously," we think, because we do not believe that Feijoo, who took imaginative liberties whenever he felt inclined, was following the logic attributed to him by the much more shortsighted Luzán. Feijoo had been describing the features of Prince Carlos and, for greater vividness, giving to each of them independent life: a stylistic trick very characteristic of the great man. ". . . His disposition had taken my side against his annoyance," said Feijoo, "and in those most tender, sovereign eyes which all the time recorded graciousness, it seemed that Compassion was laughing at Anger." [27]

Now here, Luzán approves, Feijoo, after personifying Disposition, Anger, and so on, must have realized that his flight of imagination was too extreme for prose and judiciously moderated his figure with the qualifying *"seemed,"* as Cicero would have done. It may be that Feijoo did indeed sense the need of that moderating word. A much simpler explanation is that it was merely a convenient introduction to a natural comparison and was not really to Luzán's point.[28] In truth, so immersed was Don Ignacio in his own preoccupation with formal Rhetoric that he could believe it needed scant reflection on the part of Lope's admirers to make them eventually agree with Lope's critics and admit that idols are not infallible. For his part, Don Ignacio conceived it his mission to declare the truth, he asserted, with all the easy confidence of the reformer who believes himself to be in full possession of the truth, and not flatter those who "think it weak to change their opinions and unlearn and despise when they are old what they learned and admired when young." [29]

Out of Book II we therefore emerge with the impression that all general aspects of poetry have been thoroughly reviewed and that the Preceptist has placed his emphasis where the needs of his Age, though not necessarily the needs of other Ages, required that he should place it: on intellectual effort, on solid, new, matter for thought, on the disposal of verbal rubbish, and on the preparation for a changed, cautiously safe way of poetic life to correspond to a new way of life outside books which he himself had scarcely begun to imagine.

CHAPTER 9

The Poetics. *Book III.*
The Literary Crisis. Drama

LUZÁN'S public reputation as a critic has depended, for better
or worse, rightly or wrongly, on his assessment of drama.
This was a subject on which any Spaniard, of any social or intellectual class, was ready to speak with the strength of his compelling experience. Neoclassical reform in the theaters would
often be opposed by actors and by a cross-section of their public:
all of which Luzán even as relatively unfledged as he was in
1737, knew perfectly well. So that already, over the course of the
first two books, he had attempted gradually to undermine his
Spanish readers' confidence in their own tastes.

Most of Book III is devoted to Tragedy, partly because in
Aristotle's system of aesthetic priorities Tragedy was the highest
form of drama, and in his unfinished treatise had occupied him
almost exclusively; partly because many Neoclassical principles
were applicable to all forms of drama, allowing comedy, therefore, to be dismissed briefly; partly because Luzán, as we have
seen from several contexts, believed, not unreasonably, that the
time had come, for aesthetic as well as moral reasons, to explore
the wider possibilities of rational sobriety.

The different forms of drama were understood by Neoclassicists,
Luzán included, to be due to different ways in which a poet
"imitates"—that problematic Aristotelian word which will give
even more trouble in our dramatic thinking than it has given
in its lyrical usage. Luzán rightly recognizes the word to represent one of the most significant concepts in Aristotle's definition
of drama. And having traced the history of Tragedy—incidentally
discussing its name, associated with singing and dancing and
with the dramatic evolution of the Chorus, and mentioning vari-

ous theories about its development—he advances towards his main task of seeking the whole meaning of Tragic Imitation.

I   *The Problem of Tragic "Imitation"*

Asking ourselves the same question as Aristotle and the more observant of the Neoclassicists asked themselves, we might try to discover if our basic conception of what is "tragic" is the same as theirs and so if, basically, the Classical conception remains true for all time; in other words, if Luzán represents a permanently realistic ideology. It would probably be agreed that what we now understand as a tragedy, in any sense of that word, involves some disaster, commonly, though perhaps not invariably to modern ideas, on a large scale. We do not, instinctively at least, conceive of tragedy as a disaster occurring to a declared enemy, for the enemy's disaster is our victory and necessarily produces in us relief, satisfaction, triumph, or other primitive emotions of the kind. Consequently our conception of "tragedy" is concerned not only with disaster, but with disaster, or threat of disaster, in which our sympathies can be engaged. This last is the clause in the definition of tragedy which has caused the greatest controversy among Neoclassical critics. They were obliged by their own trained belief in the completeness of traditional explanations of philosophy to try to fit their practical observations into academic formulae already authorized; in fact to substitute an exercise in abstract logic for what moderns, inspired by many ancient masters who worked more instinctively than academically, would now call a demonstration of practical psychology.

Up to a point practical psychologists and ancient philosophers —Aristotle, at any rate—meant the same thing. It was the Neoclassicists who became obsessed with formulae. If we analyze our feelings in the presence of tragedy, we realize that we have been forced out of our nervous self-awareness by an alienating sense of shock, and have experienced a certain clearance of the nerves, some relief of temporary forgetfulness from private preoccupations and pressures, some hollowing and emptying that leaves us physically shaky. This is very close to Aristotle's description of catharsis. Again, Tragedy, we know, may function companionably as a vicarious exteriorization of our half-suppressed fears and anxieties. For probably the easiest tragedy to bear is not that of fears hidden, but rather the fears openly shared, for instance in wartime; while the tragedy most difficult to bear, and so more forceful in its effect, is the uncommunicated recognition of terror potential. It will be remembered that Aristotle's word for the release of nervous fears and passions is "purge." And in the treatment of this part of the Aristotelian definition, Luzán, for all his would-be empiricism, becomes infected by the stuffier, the more artificial atmosphere of Neoclassical variants.

To purge the spectator of his passions, the post-Aristotelians were too ready to explain, meant to rid him of wrong tendencies by the spectacle of disaster, presumably as an onlooker might be expected to be deterred from stealing and murdering by seeing some criminal hanging from a gibbet in a public place, or by feeling, even at a distance, some heat from the flames that burn him alive. Most modern Aristotelian scholars would appear to agree with Butcher [1] that this Philosopher's idea of the purgation of spectators' passions by pity for the hero's plight, by fearful anxiety for his human predicament, and by natural, perhaps almost superstitious application of another man's bad fortune to themselves, was more aesthetic than directly moral. By which, perhaps, we may understand that Aristotle's idea of dramatic purgation was of a kind of shock, exquisite in its satisfaction, more akin to pleasure than to edification, that we experience when drastic human problems, exteriorized on the stage, cause us emotionally to recognize for what it is some undefined or half-suppressed problem—fear of our own. Aristotle, Butcher assures us, did not regard the theater in itself as a School of Morals,[2] and any lesson to be derived would not, to his mind, derive from an ethical ideal of conduct, but from the human pity and fear inspired by momentous inevitabilities.[3] As for "purgation," Butcher instances the highly plausible theory, discussed in 1857 by Jacob Bernays, who based it on a Renaissance theory of catharsis. According to this version, Aristotle, whose knowledge covered medical fields, thought of "purgation" in a medical sense, and interpreted the means of producing it by medical analogies.[4] For the ancient pharmaceutical belief was that certain kinds of physical disorders are cured by purgative medicines with chemical properties similar to those inherent in the disorder, and so which oppose like to like: that is, for instance, certain sour things cure various sour or acid complaints; emotion, is cured by emotions "like in kind but not identical." [5] This would mean evidently that dramatic catharsis contributes not so much to a cure of particular passions as to pleasurable relief from the nervous suppression and accumulation of passions in general, and bears some relation, in kind if not in degree, to the relief given by violence in physical exercise to the violence of suppressed emotions.

Aristotle's definition of tragedy, or at least the nearest he comes to a definition, while including most of the terms which, taken out of their context lend themselves to obscurity—imitation, a "certain magnitude," purgation of the passions by pity and fear— is broad and very general. In Butcher's translation it runs:

"Tragedy, then, is an imitation of an action that is serious, complete, and of a certain magnitude; in language embellished with each kind of artistic ornament, the several kinds being found in separate parts of the play; in the form of action, not of narrative; through pity and fear effecting the proper purgation of these emotions." [6]

Undeniably this is a definition crying out for elucidation, and Luzán's concern is, as usual, to gather examples of disagreement among critics in order that no possibility may be overlooked. By the time he evolved his own definition, he would therefore have taken into account the differing views of major interpreters on the meaning of Aristotle's elaboration of his own statements. It was not an unreasonable method of working. Nevertheless, since Luzán and his modern authorities were scarcely the first to use it, they were working on elaborations of elaborations which in fact had already changed Aristotelian reflection into pointed instruction. Don Ignacio's anxiously explicit definition is as follows:

"Tragedy is a dramatic representation of a great change of fortune suffered by kings, princes, and personages of high quality and (social) dignity whose fall from power, whose deaths, adversities, and dangers may so promote terror and compassion in the soul of the spectator that he is cured and purged of these and other passions, and that (the experience) may serve as an example and lesson to all, but especially to kings and persons of superior authority and power." [7] Which immediately changes the original emphasis from a statement of experience to a moral recommendation.

II *Plot-Soul and Plot-Body*

"The plot, then, is the first principle, and, as it were, the soul of a Tragedy" (Aristotle).[8]

This startling pronouncement explains the precedence and general importance given by Neoclassicists to the word translated variously and confusingly as *plot* or *theme* through the Latin *fabula*, literally *fable*. Indirectly it is the reason why consideration of "plot" figures in Luzán's treatise on drama as early as Chapter II and why it spreads urgently over several chapters more. Aristotle's strange words—strange, that is, to those who missed the wholeness of Aristotelian thought by concentrating on individual phrases—inevitably led to controversy over the meaning of words. Luzán, therefore, first discusses some of the problems involved in such controversies, then reviews the various forms that "plots" may take, and in Chapter IV reaches the more intricate subject of plot-integrity, or the Neoclassical version of what Aristotle called "completeness" of action.[9]

What Aristotle, the scientist, meant, he himself explains, though in terms which later Preceptists treated too superficially. The word translated usually as "plot," sometimes as "fable," does not refer solely in its Aristotelian context, Butcher stresses, to the "story" or outline of subject matter, but to a dynamic organism of action—as we might say, perhaps, a unit of mental and emotional stress caught in its state of process, and displaying an intrinsic inevitability of consequences, the active fact of a human reality. At any rate, Butcher convincingly assures us, from the large Aristotelian context, that "plot" in Aristotle's understanding "implies a conflict" and "embraces not only the deeds, the incidents, the situations, but also the mental processes and the motives which underlie the outward events or which result from them." "We may even modify Aristotle's phrase," Butcher elaborates, and "say that the dramatic conflict, not the mere plot, is the soul of a tragedy." Aristotle's "plot," then, is an "animating principle," the "soul," the "primary and moving force" in the body of the tragedy.[10]

Presumably the new Classicists had vaguely caught a distant glimpse of Aristotle's meaning. Presumably, like Aristotle himself, they were to some extent aware of the flamelike intensity of Greek inspiration. But, unlike Aristotle, they could not philosophically appreciate the ultimate significance of what they distantly saw. At least they could not reduce the full significance of what they saw to a formal system on paper. They focused their attention, consciously frustrated, it may be, upon externals: the type of theme, the social and moral range of characters, the organization of those tangible circumstances which had been discussed incidentally by their Greek master.

Aristotle's realism is less restricted than that of his disciples whose conception of plot is rather of a material body than of a living principle: a body with classifiable members performing related and readily classifiable functions. Among these disciples, Luzán, working obviously in his natural element, shows manifest enjoyment in his self-imposed task of cataloguing different kinds of plot-bodies, providing them with descriptive titles, systematically assigning to each its proper members with their proper functions, and arranging theories about them into suitable categories. The mere ordering of material often prompts illuminating questions, and Luzán was interested to discuss any comprehensive theory to which aesthetic administration led him. But, with the rest of his Preceptist colleagues, he was more successful in his interpretation of the minor externals of Greek models of tragedy than he was in the interpretation of their major impact.

It was the ambiguity produced by academic use of the Latin *fabula* which gave undue prominence to the principle of moral instruction. When discussing its semantic derivation, Luzán explains that it had suggested something neutral between "truth and falsehood," that it had been used in Latin in the sense of either *fact* or *fiction*, that drama had been called *fabula* and that, by a combination of all these possibilities, the word had acquired for most theorists the meaning of "subject"—that is, the story or plot of a tragedy. He particularly approves, however, of a school of thought represented by Le Bossu, which sees in *fabula* the establishment of the moral law regarded by Luzán as the prime motive force of drama. *Fabula*, which had been used of Aesop's fables, must involve, Le Bossu and those who shared his opinion had assumed, some kind of moral allegory. Therefore Luzán records Le Bossu's definition of the disputed word as: "a discourse invented with the aim of instilling good habits of life, by means of instruction under the disguise of allegory," and his rider that the essential parts of a *fabula* are the moral truth it teaches and the fiction with which that truth is disguised. This version Luzán seems able to accept without reservation and uses it as the climax of his Chapter II.

"So that (dramatic) action, alone, without allegory or instruction, is like a body without a soul, and moral instruction without imitative action to contain and conceal such instruction, is like a soul without a body." [11]

Such was the prosaic tomb of Neoclassicism in which the vitality of Aristotle had been buried.

Since tragedy for whatever reason imitated life, the plot, Aristotle thought, and his disciples heartily agreed, must be intimately concerned with human passions. Especially, Neoclassicists specified, mindful of Aristotle's argument about purgation, especially must it be the business of tragedy to move and correct the passions, through fear or pity, by the imitation of horrible and piteous misfortunes befalling kings and other conspicuously placed potentates. As if Don Ignacio had not already stressed the moral application sufficiently in Chapter II, he took the opportunity again in Chapter III of recasting even more emphatically the statement of Le Bossu that he had just recorded. Indeed he seemed unable to leave the subject alone, perhaps for the reason that Spanish drama, to its artistic credit, as posterity now thinks, had commonly left the moral, at least during the course of the play, to take care of itself, sometimes in implicit casualness, sometimes in ambiguity . It could certainly be pointed out to Luzán by those who criticized his *Poetics* that the majority of Golden Age dramatists strictly observed moral principles in the general intention of their plays, and that their serious drama, directly or indirectly, had very powerful methods of purging the emotions in the full Aristotelian sense. But Neoclassicists assumed that the "moral" message should be less confusingly inexplicit than it had been in either Spanish or English drama. And as far as Luzán was concerned, he was probably right to assume for his own times—the qualification of period is supremely important—that a rational, materialistic, literal-minded age required explicitly rational principles to ensure that logic was seen to be logical. He was also right in sensing, for he could not put his partial perception into exact words, that the Age of Reason was searching for a form of unmitigated tragedy to exteriorize its deeply troubled preoccupations. This was a more calculatedly serious—

minded era than its intuitive predecessor. By "morals" Luzán often meant responsible seriousness. Let us allow him therefore to stress his earnest thoughts again:

The *fabula* must be "that action which the poet imitates and reproduces with the idea of concealing in it some special moral instruction, and this he does by attributing such an action to certain people at a certain time, in a certain place, and in circumstances either wholly invented by the poet (as happens in comedies and certain tragedies) or taken from history completely, partially or in the mere use of historical names." [12]

Because the themes of model Greek tragedy had been concerned with misfortunes of distinguished families of antiquity, and because Aristotle had approved of historical subjects for tragic drama, the Neoclassicists found natural cause for debate in questions arising over the proportion in which fact, and the poet's interpretation of or departure from fact, should be combined. Some Neoclassicists had unimaginatively assumed that modern tragedy would continue to make use of traditional Greek and Roman themes. Others were ready to believe that subjects taken from the national histories of modern civilizations and representing modern principles would be more effective and appropriate to modern minds. Luzán, it is pleasant to report, was one of the latter, and his pronouncements on the best use of historical material are thoroughly realistic. Not for nothing was this Preceptist to become a member of Spain's Royal Academy of History. His interest in history for its own academic sake is evident from his early publications. Moreover, several of his friends, Montiano y Luyando and Eugenio de Llaguno for example, were also to become members of the Academy. Montiano, for his part, was to put into practice the principles of Neoclassical reform by publishing two tragedies on historical subjects, one of them introducing Ataulpho, a Gothic king of the Peninsula [13] about whom Luzán discoursed before the Academy. [14]

Partly, then, out of his personal interest in historical studies Luzán was to enter the debate armed with factual knowledge of details and able to express himself both with patently first-hand understanding and with more common sense than some of his Preceptist colleagues. According to their reading of Aristotle, Neoclassicists believed, with a faith ascribable to some sacred law, that for tragedy to be a genuinely artistic imitation it must contain within its historical argument some form of invention. The very word drama, ran their confession of faith, implied such a requirement. Wherefore they raised a largely artificial problem as to the exact form and position which the inventive material should take and occupy. Some of Luzán's Chapters III and IV is devoted to a recapitulation of the argument in general and to the traditional conclusion that poetry, of its moral nature, should be less concerned with what heroes actually did than with what they ought to have done, and that invention should enter the gap stretching between the actual and the potential.

One of the several indications that Luzán had been busily engaged in working out for himself the principles involved in the use of historical subject matter, is the fact that he had searched for Spanish examples with which to apply the Rules. On the one hand, agreeing with the Aristotelian recommendation that verisimilar invention is preferable to inverisimilar fact, and with the French Academy's objection to Corneille's *Le Cid* on the grounds that, though meant to be historical it looked improbable, and that not all historical truths are suitable for public performance, he searches for a Spanish parallel and produces, fairly enough, the *Ilustre Antona García (Illustrious Antona García)*, presumably in the version of Tirso de Molina. This is, one must confess, a very disconcerting play about a bossy, mannish, peasant-heroine, who historically, so it would seem, leads men into battle, who is pregnant during the critical action of the play, and who, with notorious lack of refinement, cries out in labor pains in Act III before hurrying to have her baby offstage. Critics, far more permissive than Luzán, would have found this drama embarrassingly indelicate. The fact that a good actress could bring it to startling psychological life was beside their point.

On the other hand, Luzán's suggested heroes who might suitably be borrowed from Spanish history to act as parallels to the heroes of Greek tragedy are all striking individuals in their own right: The tragic Roderick the Goth who lost Spain to the Moors in 711; the Cid—one hopes in more lifelike circumstances than those emotionalized in Corneille's *Le Cid;* Hernán Cortés, conqueror of Mexico; The Great Captain, Gonzalo de Córdoba, creator of the distinguished Spanish infantry. Luzán, then, was not a man timorously to cling to Greek and Roman models in every respect; and he had difficulty in understanding other Preceptists who condemned recourse to national, modern history as either anti-Aristotelian or antiartistic. Here Luzán's orientation was Spanish. National themes of history, ancient or relatively modern, which Neoclassical reformers tried out during the eighteenth century, did not in Spain meet with the obstacles of prejudice which they encountered sometimes in France. Subject-wise, the Neoclassical themes of Spanish history were the most acceptable features, possibly the only acceptable features, of reformist tragedy.

As for the introduction of the fictitious element into historical themes, Luzán regards it and illuminatingly explains it as part of the technical "economy" [15] of plot. If a historian, he says knowledgeably, were dealing with the Greek subject of Oedipus, he would straightforwardly begin his narrative by saying that Oedipus was the son of Laïus and Jocasta. But the dramatist, whose aim is to excite wonder and delight, and who is concerned not with facts in themselves, but with their universal significance, inventively keeps this relationship hidden from all characters until the end in order to produce a greater emotional effect on the audience. The "economy" of the plot, therefore, is the poet's lawfully artistic convenience, that disposition of events "which the poet adapts to the rules of drama as owner and absolute lord over his subject." [16] Luzán's explanation is a good and practical one and he develops it a little by showing how other fictitious elements may judiciously be introduced to improve on nature: the different temperaments given to different characters, the very selectivity and significant arrangement of episodes, the explanation of particular actions which history either does not know or is silent about. All such things, he says, are the inventions of the poet who "works and improves on the (raw) material he has borrowed from history, giving it a new form and a new life by means of his art and inventiveness." [17] Obviously Luzán's own intimacy with historical problems and material—most strikingly the historical silences of which he was to speak in his Discourse on Ataulpho to the Academy of History [18]—had fired his imagination and given him a certain interior understanding.

Another debate into which Luzán enters with personal zest concerns the technique of plot making. Aristotle, to the satisfaction of Neoclassicists, who liked talk about practical management, had submitted a factual plan for the making of a plot in historical tragedy. "As for the story, whether the poet takes it ready-made or constructs it for himself, he should first sketch its general outline, and then fill in the episodes and amplify in detail."[19] After which business-like suggestion, Aristotle goes on to explain that, once names are given to the characters, the episodes may be filled out, and that these episodes must be relevant to the action. The rest of his suggestions concern the distribution of incidents, the development of the plot, and the *dénouement*. These are general recommendations, illustrative rather than dictatorial and specific; yet it is easy to see how readily they would lend themselves to particular development.

We should observe that Luzán, still taking his bearings from historical studies, was uneasy at certain modern tendencies to overspecify where Aristotle had generalized, and he politely differed from Le Bossu on this subject. The Frenchman is dogmatic. Let the dramatist, he says, prepare his plot by working out initially a basis of moral instruction. Let him next reduce his moral to an action, general in nature in the first instance, and imitated from the true actions of men. Then finally, let him search in history for a corresponding action to disguise his instruction, and let him then furnish it with the right names and details.[20]

Luzán may not have been remarkable as a creative artist. But he was artist enough, apparently, to know that Le Bossu's teaching was more relevant to the critics' world than to the world of poets. Therefore, while welcoming system and order in Le Bossu's aesthetics, especially, he says, for comedy, which he places on a more prosaic plane than tragedy, he doubts the wisdom or naturalness of Le Bossu's methodical prescription. Its wisdom he doubts, because tragedy in its own right has already been established as the purger of passions and accordingly does not require an additional moral. Its naturalness he doubts, because he is not convinced that the masters really followed any such method. Don Ignacio's doubts are precious evidence of a certain independence of judgment. They show also that vaguely he, too, expects tragedy to project its force by internal rather than by external means. In which respect he is not very typical of his century. They also show that Luzán's own artistic instincts—humble though they might be—have enabled him to understand that a poet takes shortcuts through reason, such shortcuts as mere critics cannot be expected to anticipate. Don Ignacio certainly holds Le Bossu in much respect and now goes out of his way to say so. At the same time he firmly asserts that when poets are preparing to write historical tragedy, they are likely to find it natural first to go for inspiration to history itself, leaving the inherent moral, Luzán implies, to grow from within the subject. His rejection of a moral imposed by the poet from outside his subject may seem a small matter. For some form of moral, at all costs, there must be. Nevertheless, in its limited context, the objection may be said to constitute a minor triumph for artistic good sense.

The remaining qualities which Aristotle thought desirable for his plot-soul, "completeness" and "greatness," Luzán treats in the main with fussy pedantry and disappointing literalness. Aristotle's advice about balanced development, his explicit references to a properly coordinated beginning, middle, and end to give the effect of "completeness" [21] encouraged Neoclassicists to dally busily in trifles and simplicities. They were liable to satisfy themselves with elementary speculation as to where, precisely, a beginning should turn into a middle and a middle into an end. Also they tended to regard as a problem of exquisite subtlety the related question as to whether or no a poet has a right to reverse the natural, chronological order of any human action and reveal the motive-beginning of the plot only after the audience has been plunged into the middle.

Luzán offers no exception to the Neoclassical tendency to oversimplify the intensity of proportionate completeness by dogmatizing on elementary externals. But his reversion to the metaphor of sculpture in these circumstances is at least imaginative. He is reminded of that untreated block of marble—the equivalent of some block of history—from which an artist cuts and separates off only that special piece which claims his interest and which conforms to the size and proportion of the statue he has in mind. It is true that Luzán often walked through the minutiae of aesthetics with his eyes on the ground. But whenever he lifted his head to contemplate some example of great artistic achievement of which he could conscientiously approve, he seemed to acquire new vision, and, in his own quiet way, to glory in the full force of the full effect of that achievement.

Nor does Luzán offer any exception to the habit of misunderstanding Aristotle's meaning of "greatness" of plot. Like his fellow Neoclassicists, he was wont either to repeat Aristotle's words, or to extend his own commentary over the most obvious and concrete aspects of Aristotle's explanation. Butcher, meditating on this question of "greatness" of plot, credits Aristotle with a subtlety which would be well beyond Neoclassical understanding. For he believes, with a confidence made reasonable by the Greek context, that Aristotle's conception of "greatness" and integrity of plot was related to his conception of dramatic power and tension, having more to do with interior quality than with external management.[22]

Altogether one might say that on the profound and complicated subject of the motor-vitality of plot-soul Luzán was content to exchange surface formalities with his Neoclassical kind. On some other plot-issues about which he had special knowledge—the treatment of history, for example—he was inclined to apply the test of his own experience to other people's opinions. On certain points he was ready to exert his independent judgment in support of a poet's rights. At odd moments he might transcend formal reasoning and leap to a higher plane of intuition.

III The "Superstition" of the Unities [23]

One of the most debated principles of plot construction and management was the so-called Aristotelian Theory of the Unities. The reason for the vigor and extensiveness of this debate is largely that nonobservance of these Unities was one of the most obvious ways in which Spanish and English dramatists diverged from the Classical norm. It was also a matter on which, with a minimum of philosophical or dramatic knowledge, a critic could argue to his heart's content and believe all the while that he talked profoundly. For it must not be supposed that Aristotle's disciples had defined the inner significance, the inner dramatic power, of which the Unities—one or three as the case might be—were the outward and visible signs.

Aristotle's thoughts on Unity were bound up with his conception of dynamic conflict and refer to an action given universal significance, a "complete" action, "unit" of action, or, in literal translation of his own word, an action "according to the whole," a "unification" for the sake of "significance," [24] "the principle," explains Butcher, "of limit, without which an object loses itself in . . . the region of the undefined." [25] Aristotle, in the interests of dramatic power, was rightly obsessed with the effect of intensive concentration. But, as Neoclassicists generally knew, the Unity of Action was the only Unity he had insisted upon.

The "superstition of the Unities," as Butcher calls the commandment to observe the three Unities of Action, Time, and Place, was derived from the deductions or imaginations of much lesser men than Aristotle, notably commentators of Horace, who carried external logic as far as it would go. Aristotle's *Poetics* contained texts that could be manipulated to fit many sectarian purposes. It is obvious enough that Aristotle, for his part, appreciated economy in dramatic time—evidently because the Greek dramatists he knew and on whom he based his analysis were themselves economic in the use of the time factor. But the "Unity of Time" explicitly formulated as a commandment, depended, we need to remember, on a mistranslation of a passage in the *Poetics* which literally is:

"Tragedy endeavors, *as far as possible* (italics mine), to confine itself to a single revolution of the sun, or but slightly to exceed this limit; whereas the Epic action has no limit of time." [26] The reference, then, was to a tendency in Greek practice which was converted into a convenient law, "as far as possible" being translated into various words of definite injunction. Unity of Place was added for good measure:

"Did Aristotle take note of a tendency towards concentration? Instantly, though he never so much as mentioned 'unity of place,' they (the new arbiters) ordered playwrights to keep all their action in a single place." [27]

The "Superstition" of the Unities is an aspect of aesthetic faith which, quite apart from its connection with the supposed authority of an infallible Aristotle, has a particular bearing on the study of eighteenth-century mentality. Butcher comments on the role it played in general as a "fallacious" principle of "deception," [28] that is to say, in the exaggerated interests of stage illusion. For our own purposes we are concerned with the particular role it played in the eighteenth century's material understanding of what was dramatically lifelike. Now rightly, now wrongly, the realistic mind of eighteenth-century intellectuals, Neoclassical or otherwise, regarded stage performances with scientific literalness. The practical observers of the Age of Reason cared more than their predecessors if actors spoke their lines unconvincingly, if they giggled in corners when they should have been attending to the business of the play, if historical drama was historically in-accurate, if characters delivered themselves of unnatural senti-ments or used phraseology not belonging to their social class, if scenery and costumes were inappropriate to the dramatic cir-cumstances. It was in the eighteenth century supremely that the idea of complete stage illusion was carried by theater observers to its extreme limits. For these new critics, the creed of The Three Unities seemed to be supported by the evidence of practical ob-servation and plain common sense. Never before, perhaps, had the Unities been regarded so empirically. It is in this light, there-fore, that we must view Luzán's calculated and not unreasonable acceptance of them.

It should also be said that in systematizing Aristotle the Neo-classicists, admittedly dictating where he had merely observed and advised, were not drawing notoriously unnatural conclusions, however erroneous we may think them, when they preached the Unities as revealed facts. Instinctively they regarded a reduction in time and space as a corollary to Aristotle's request for dramatic concentration, and generally assumed that it would allow the emphasis of a play to rest on the thought, or moral message, instead of on incident or sentiment. The eighteenth century in-wardly craved for dramas of serious reasoning, and was ready, obscurely, as we see from Luzán's translation of La Chaussée, to study the drama of mental behaviorism. The merely temporary value of the Neoclassicists' recommendations certainly did not lie in any general principle of concentrated dramatic tension, though their explanation of the phenomenon of tension was in-adequate and they could not legislate for it by relying on three Unities. Their merely temporary value lay rather in the fact that they judged outsize and unconventional art as inferior, and that they considered themselves judges instead of aesthetic historians and analysts. This was an attitude provocative of controversy, especially in a country devoted to the individuality of its own artistic customs.

Luzán's considered opinion on the subject of the Unities runs broadly as follows. He agrees that the Aristotelian *Poetics* is at best fragmentary, and that the master's meaning is frequently obscure. He believes, after reviewing the consensus of opinion of commentators and critics, and after studying Aristotle for him-self, that it is right to take the strictest interpretation, and that the ideal length of time represented by the play should not exceed the time taken for that play to be performed. Likewise he believes that the place represented in the plot should not change at all; that the action should be free from any matter not immediately and necessarily concerned with it; and that it should be directed at every point to the complete unity of the whole.

The Unity of Action seemed the easiest of the three to interpret because Aristotle had described it explicitly as a Unity, and obviously had been impressed by the pressure which economic tension produced on an audience. Any doubts expressed by Luzán, in consultation with other authorities, are concerned with side issues though chiefly in respect of the Epic, somewhat unsuitably invited into this chapter, rather than of drama. He doubts, for example, if Unity can be said to exist where one man is involved in many actions; and he decides with Aristotle that Unity must be envisaged, not in relation to a particular person, but to the dramatic action.[29] This contention, of course, challenges the Golden Age tradition of the chronicle-play. And a modern critic could only agree with Luzán on the general soundness of the theory itself. There are Spanish and English chronicle-plays which fail to sustain a dramatic effect. There are, however, many Spanish and English chronicle-plays which make throughout their course a very powerful effect indeed and produce overall a curiously unified impact of events and personalities. So that most critics today would feel that if chronicle-plays can prove themselves successful, they have a right to be artistically respected, Unity or no. However, from the point of view of the Classicists' need for an explicit rule of artistic life, it was safe and reasonable for them to assert that dramatic force was more likely to be produced by strict external unity than otherwise. Even most apologists of Golden Age practice found the Unity of Action fairly acceptable. At least it was the least unpopular of the three.

The Unity of Time, on the contrary, lent itself to controversy among the very Neoclassicists, not indeed as a general claim, but in the problem it posed as to how strictly those claims should be exercised. Here, ironically, Aristotle gave little help. He had mentioned that Greek dramatists customarily confined the action to a *revolution of the sun*, provoked wasteful quarrelling over the meaning of the *revolution* or *period*, as it was sometimes translated, and raised advocates of clamorously rival claims for a dramatic time of anything from twelve to forty-eight hours, favorite "periods" being twelve hours and twenty-four. Where so much had been agitatedly said on the extension or reduction of a few hours here or there, Luzán's conclusion has the ring of common sense. It would be logical, he thought, to assume that Aristotle's imperfect text, even as it stands, could refer, not just to a whole period of sun, of, for example, twelve hours, but to some part of a day. Why not, therefore, assume that the play must cover the least possible time, ideally—for he does make allowance for necessary deviations—about three hours, or roughly the actual length of the performance? [30]

Here a critic who is used to economic timing in modern dramas would be likely to sympathize with Luzán's general findings, though he would be unlikely to sympathize with every detail of the Preceptist's full argument. It is true to assert, as does Luzán, that the equating of the dramatist's time with real time is a close imitation of life and therefore highly acceptable artistically. But the corollary is not in reality as convincing as it seemed to Luzán's reason. It is absurd, supposes Don Ignacio, with much Neoclassical backing, to think that an audience can verisimilarly imagine more time to have passed than has actually transpired. For an audience should be looking at a drama as a person looks through a window, at things that are concurrently happening in the street.[31] Only a critic trained to Neoclassical ideas and used to performances of Neoclassical drama almost exclusively, as was Luzán in 1737, could honestly attribute to audiences the limitations of his own literalness.

When Luzán came to discuss the Unity of Place, his reasoning about its qualifying clauses operated in reverse: a most instructive demonstration of circumstances altering cases. As in debates over the Unity of Time, he endorsed the views of those who interpreted this third principle of Unity strictly. Not that Aristotle had made any ruling here. But his silence had been variously interpreted. And Luzán sensibly thought that if the Unity of Place constructed from the alluring gaps in Aristotle's notes was to have any meaning, it should not permit even minor changes of scene. Here was another delicate subject, territory not less "hazardous," [32] warns Luzán, than that of Action and Time. One outstanding difference now, however, is that Luzán is disposed, surprisingly in face of his strictures over Time, to admit certain concessions.

At first it seems remarkable that someone, who can believe it is difficult for an audience to accept imaginatively the artificial passage of time, should think it possible for the same audience to accept artificial changes in place. Surely a sense of time is more naturally indefinite and illusory than a sense of place, less solid, less circumstantial. Yet, while Luzán in 1737 had had scant opportunity for exercising imagination over the passage of time in performances of Spanish plays, he was not without experience in maneuverability of stage place. The Unity of Place had been gently stretched by Italy's favorite writer of the century, Metastasio, and Luzán would be well used to minor changes of scene. Also let us remember that he belonged to a small minority of reformist Spaniards who were worried by lack of scenery in Spanish theaters. As a man of imagination, he was appreciative of material decoration, and Place can be more plastically represented than Time. Apparently, then, his interest in pictorial art directed his attention to stage backcloths and decoration. Italian sets for opera often suggested a composite scene linking different parts of a town or place. Luzán was unwilling to stretch the Place Unity by the old, invisible Spanish method of having no scenery at all. He found that absurd. But he was ready to consider ways and means of narrowing the distance between different places by a kind of physical *trompe-l'oeil*, by some such method, for instance, as Baruffaldi's simultaneous settings.[33]

Stage divisions, horizontal or vertical, seemed to Luzán in 1737 a happy solution to the problem of monotony, and he discussed Baruffaldi's suggestions enthusiastically. In his Italian experience of scenic custom it would require no excessive feat of imagination to accept the telescoping of places. The stabilizing influence in the imaginative exercise was the concrete scenery itself. Even so, he was sufficiently cautious to recommend tests and experiments before putting Baruffaldi's idea into practice. Moreover, as we have suggested, he may personally have conducted some such experiments in the performance of his heroic drama, *Virtue Crowned,* before deciding that the practical effect was less verisimilar than he had expected; and it may well be for this reason that he reduced his advocacy of the technique in 1789 edition to the size of a mere reference.

IV *The Plot in Motion: a "Multitude of Doubts"*

So far Luzán has been discussing the static constituents of drama: the aims, the themes, and the unified structure. Now he begins to consider the development of activity once the plot is set in motion, the episodes leading to changes of fortune which are to purge the audience's passions, the types and temperaments of characters acting as agents of purgation. To passion, purgation, and characters he will return in more detail later. For the moment, in Chapter VI he pauses to review a "multitude of doubts" [34] which his predecessors had voiced about dramatic action and activity.

The first doubt is one of interpretation. Did Aristotle contradict himelf when, indicating in one place that he preferred complex action, he said, in another, that simple action is better? It is unnecessary to follow all the details of this argument. But it is significant that when Luzán adds his vote to those who favor the opinion that Aristotle preferred complexity, a deciding factor is his conviction that complex action is more "marvelous" and that he would expect Aristotle to favor it for this reason. When using the word "marvelous," Luzán was employing a technical term of Neoclassical aesthetics which would be more limited in meaning than is the overworked word in English. Marvels of plot would not normally refer to the supernatural or anything of an external nature. Rather the word would signify, for instance, those startling genealogical revelations of Greek tragedy and other reverses or coincidences inherent in extraordinary situations of human irony. As for the question of whether Aristotle was contradicting himself or not, Luzán wisely attributes apparent contradiction to the confused phraseology of translators. Other conspicuous "doubts" he mentions refer to the dramatic changes of fortune designed to inspire pity and terror, and the type of characters involved in tragic demonstration. Of course, Don Ignacio's doubts were shallow. He was much less aware of the ultimate significance of all these subjects than Aristotle had been. But he was at least as aware as most of the disputants, with the possible exception of disputant playwrights like Corneille.

It was the latter he reported sympathetically in Chapter VI when discussing Aristotle's choice of an ideal hero as a man neither good nor bad, and the kind of disaster conducive to pity and fear. Corneille had created imposingly "good," martyr-heroes whom Luzán evidently admired. Once more, therefore, he is to be found on the side of those who "doubt" the precept, or the text of the master. Corneille, from the breadth and depth of his stage experience, disagreed with Aristotle's requirement that a tragic hero should come to grief, not through the commission of some great crime, but through ignorance or a minor fault. To most Neoclassical critics also, major faults were unacceptable in tragic heroes. For how, it was asked, could a criminal induce pity? Usually Preceptists were more ready to take the word of other Preceptists than that of successful playwrights who were closely in touch with theater audiences. Corneille knew very well that, properly handled, both good and bad characters, both happy and unhappy issues out of affliction, both martyr-deaths and criminal-deaths, can shake spectators into moral thought, force them to share in the sense of guilt of those whose vices are enlargements of their own petty ones, and feel compassion for innocent suffering as depicted in his moving *Polyeucte.* This was the experience of a practitioner. And Luzán, apparently impressed, allowed the French playwright to voice his well-based opinions uninterruptedly, even it would seem, to claim preferential treatment. Naturally all disputants were putting undue stress on Aristotle's recommendation. But Corneille was right to disagree with those who tied Aristotle to one possibility only; and Luzán, in the general noise of controversy and amid the "multitude of doubts," was right to listen to a dramatist. Incidentally, in legislating for changes of fortune and the means by which these are to be achieved, he applauded the ingenuity of the Spanish playwright, Moreto. For he was not reluctant to give praise to Spanish dramatists where he thought it was due.

This section of Book III, as well as any portion of Luzán's work, displays his potentialities as a practical teacher. He has the teacher's technique of arranging instruction in orderly sequence, of breaking up general ideas into easily comprehensible component parts, and illustrating each part with concrete examples; of repeating key ideas in different contexts; of recapitulating the argument at intervals; of preparing the mind with introductory remarks and of pressing conclusions; of organizing analysis so that the reader knows what is to be done before the operation starts; of treating exceptions to a rule in unconfusingly subordinate positions. When in Chapter VII he begins to instruct poets on the Aristotelian technique of plot making, he seems to be comfortably established in his pedagogic stride. The analogies he offers for the poet's practical guidance are singularly well chosen. Different episodes, he explains, are like seeds in a plant body, different from each other but equally essential to the plant. Some are small, and some are large, but they grow in right proportion with the plant and with each other. He takes the trouble to dissect the plot and its seed-episodes both in Classical models—the epic story of Ulysses, or the *Iphigenia in Tauris* of Euripides, and in the Spannish *¿Cuál es la mejor perfección . . . ? (Which is greater Perfection . . . ?)* of Calderón.[35] His demonstration of common faults, or what to him were faults, in the making of soul-plots, is also organized with a certain imagination and skill. Among the faults, we are not surprised to find Spanish misdemeanors figuring largely: deliberate violation of the Rules and deliberate efforts, so Luzán assumed, to please spectators with external "marvels." Naturally, Don Ignacio was oversimplifying a very complex artistic phenomenon. There were Spanish examples in which "marvels" were cheaply produced for effect, and fell below artistic levels. There were others in which "marvels" were deliberately produced for effect, yet raised in artistic tone to full or near-sublimity. One of his own major defects was precisely this tendency to generalize. Nevertheless, in so far as he was instructing hopeful dramatists of his own century, his strictures by no means would come amiss.

A last chapter (VIII) on the subject of dramatic "soul" discusses crises of intrigue and ideal solutions. Again, it is Luzán's meticulousness which is most impressive: details of how arrangements for the crises should be made, and at which points crises should arise and suspense increase. But this subject introduced a line of thought along which, out of loyalty to Aristotle, Luzán arrived at an oddly untenable position and illustrated the danger of defining from theoretic knowledge only. He had been speaking of tragic solutions, and decided, from Aristotle's text, over which he was consciously puzzled, that a genuine solution could only be a happy one, since solution, by definition, must indicate the way in which a hero overcomes his difficulties. Just possibly, he was scrupulous enough to reflect, the term *enredo*, or complication, might sometimes unsuitably be given to the hero's efforts to con-

serve or augment his happiness from the beginning of the play
to the *peripeteia,* or that moment when the action changes course,
and the solution in this instance would be his failure. Of course
the argument is purely academic, with little bearing on the practice of the Greeks, Romans, or modern tragedians. At the same
time, let us not forget that to Neoclassical Preceptists, and most
Neoclassical practitioners, academic argument was supremely important as a means leading to the end of academic authority, just
as disputation in Academies of Languages, or among compilers
of standard dictionaries, is still expected to lead to authoritative
conclusions. Besides, the vital consideration here was rather the
correct understanding of Aristotle than strict dictation to dramatists. On this rare occasion Spanish playwrights emerge from the
polemic swirling academically around them in a glow of Neoclassical approval. They are praised by Luzán for their happy
knack of inventing complications and solutions. Don Ignacio's
sense of proportion, too, enables him to realize that ability to
maintain dramatic suspense as one crisis of the plot leads to another is an enviable art to be cultivated with the utmost as-
siduity.

V *Pathos in Practice, and the Characters Who Engender It*

Already, in various ways, Luzán had anticipated his discourse
in Chapter IX on the passions to be dramatically purged and the
characters best suited for dramatic instruction. By now he is ready
to examine the matter thoroughly, and both with regard to
spectators' passions and to characters who purge them, he is to
be seen at the top of his empiric form.

First his review of the interpretations of Aristotle's somewhat
Delphic pronouncements on this subject shows Luzán how
broadly based and so how deeply worthwhile the argument must
prove. Moreover, his own initial remarks in Chapter IX, that
passions are excited more effectively by visual presentation than
by second-hand description of misfortune, means that his view of
Classical drama was of drama acted: an important recognition of
Greek dramatic life which many dramatic critics neglected.

Carefully Luzán picks his way through his predecessors' opinions, testing them all against his observation of drama on the
stage and eventually taking his stand on realistic practice. Some
of Aristotle's interpreters, Beni, for instance, thought that not

only pity and terror are purged by tragedy, but all passions, and that tragedy is a powerful vehicle for shocking men of high position into moral improvement. The philosopher Iamblichus had looked at tragedy as an escape valve and had said that if passions are suppressed they will later burst out too violently, as does suppressed laughter. Corneille thought that the sight of other people's catastrophes makes a man fear that they could also happen to himself and causes him to behave more cautiously in self-defense. Robortello and the Spanish González de Salas thought that when pity and terror are excited by a character's misfortunes the spectator, thus vicariously experienced in disaster, will become steeled against the worst that can befall him. Don Ignacio applauds this last idea, for indeed it is a good one. The cultured man, particularly, is seldom shaken to the core by merely reading tragedy. He is at an academic remove from vicarious horrors because he has learned to rationalize them and know why they occurred. His knowledge of literature has familiarized him with the idea of large-scale death and disaster. Usually it takes a drama acted on the stage to shake him into realistic receptivity.

At any rate, Don Ignacio, with all his colleagues' suggestions in mind, and after weighing and judging them dispassionately, rises to one of his own best performances in the *Poetics* by bringing psychological analysis to bear on a common human experience that theatergoers of any century must have shared.

If we examine our reaction, both immediately and for some time after seeing searing tragedy in a mass-hushed, darkened theater—domestic television does not produce the same effect— we shall probably acknowledge a sensation as of physical hollowness and mental clarity. Well might the Ancients have spoken of "purging." This sensation is normally accompanied by new or renewed consciousness, so it would seem, of something either not understood before or temporarily forgotten: that fresh understanding provoked by all momentous things, and which, instead of crushing or depressing, generally subdues only to alert. We should probably agree, too, that such electrifying occasions, which are not sufficiently prolonged to produce exhaustion, have an immediate effect of sharpening our receptivity towards the serious things of life and of stilling, therefore, our more trivial agitations, at least for the time being. In the long term they often encourage the exercise of objectivity, because they have linked us with experiences outside our own. Precisely this kind of experience is realistically conjured up by Luzán when he describes the effect which a good tragedy should make on spectators and when, from his seat in the auditorium, he speaks from personal experience of the process known to the Ancients as the purging of the passions.

"Those changes of fortune, the disasters and deaths of princes and great personages cause the spectators to go out of the theater with an inner seriousness (literally *sadness*) with a lingering trace of something which is as it were both bitter and sharp, and which for awhile holds our spirit still in a melancholy and thoughtful silence." [36]

This is not the only time when Luzán has spoken of silences as positively influential.

Having now thoroughly entered into the spirit of remembered experience, which he would have regarded as a moral experience, he is able to develop his ideas the more convincingly. Wisdom, he reflects on a religious note, is seldom born of undiluted pleasure or liveliness, and he stresses thoughtfully the human need at times for the maturing experience, vicarious or otherwise, of some degree of suffering:

"There is no doubt that too much gaiety, too much attention given to external objects and the variety of (worldly) desires greatly dissipates the spirit, distracts it and so alienates it (from reality) that very seldom does it enter into itself, draw itself together to try, all by itself, to know itself, and thence, as from a (different) standpoint to know the truth of the things around it. So with that seriousness and silent recollection which tragedy leaves in the spectator, this profitable retirement of the soul into itself is accomplished, excessive gaiety is tempered, pride is mortified, and the vanity of empty hopes and useless desires is moderated." [37] Again he seems to have been meditating on mystical theology.

Chapter IX is also interesting for several other reasons. First, Luzán in this chapter argues the practical case for and against direct representation of violence on the stage. It would not have been illiberal of him to object to stage killings. Even in the most powerful dramas they seldom, of themselves, contribute to dramatic power. On the contrary, they lend themselves to grotesque mishandling and cheap histrionic virtuosity. Luzán astonishes us, therefore, by a willingness to admit them. Naturally he has weighed the matter carefully and consulted many authorities. But his conclusion is that critics had been watering down the message of Aristotle, which appeared to admit stage deaths, and he prefers to accept that message as it originally stood. Behind his own conclusion, then, is the highest authority of all. Still, he has also been thinking out the matter for himself and relates Aristotle's findings to the observed fact that dramatic action speaks louder than dramatic narration. We need hardly add that the stage killings authorized by Luzán are of a relatively circumspect nature: that is, killings by swords, daggers, poison cups, and other sophisticated or gentlemanly instruments. Tragedy was not licensed by him to indulge in primitive atrocities and in violence primarily horrific. Assuredly Don Ignacio would have been disgusted by both the quality and quantity of Shakespearian slaughter, though even the uninhibited Elizabethans usually knew where to draw the artistic line. Lesser tragedians, wallowing in barbarity on any stage, in any period, would generally be wallowing in bad taste and parting company with literature.

Secondly, there is a curious change made in the 1789 edition. Luzán had been expressing surprise that Spanish dramatists had not taken advantage of the tragic form—he meant, undiluted tragedy. In France and Italy, he observed, the value of pure tragedy had been well known. But to those two countries in 1737 he allied the name of England. This could only mean that his knowledge of English tragedy was limited to the decorous eighteenth-century *Cato* of Joseph Addison, of whom continental Neoclassicists thoroughly approved. Decidedly it would not mean that Luzán knew at first hand England's Golden Age of tragedy. The Elizabethans would have shocked him even more than the Lopeans or Calderonians. In 1789 the individual names of the three countries are eliminated and the phrase is altered to "other nations." By 1789 Elizabethan misdemeanors would be familiar to Neoclassicists in translations, recasts, or imitations, and were hardly less notorious in Neoclassical circles for being modified. This is another instance, consequently, of the limitedness of Luzán's knowledge of English literature in 1737.

VI   *Tragic Characterization*

"Manners, that is to say the disposition, the temperament and what other nations call the *character* proper to each person" [38] (Luzán).

In the interests of profoundly serious tragedy rendered sublime by elevated thought, Luzán needed no prompting from his many authorities to realize that the way to profundity led not through external events and situations, be they never so well unified, but through the subterranean mysteries of human crises of will and emotion. But that being said, it must also be admitted that the principal aim of eighteenth-century Neoclassicists was almost exclusively moral, and that, for all their would-be realism, psychological treatment of character did not enter into their calculations. The "character" important to them was "character" as theoretically it ought to be, logical to the end. They are therefore obliged to make an uneasy compromise between their own scientific inclination towards objectivity, and what they believed to be Aristotle's dictates on universality. Perhaps their most insidious misunderstanding of Aristotle's subtlety had arisen over his prescription of "good" dramatic characters.

Butcher suggests that Aristotle's conception of "good" heroes has much in common with our modern conception of "greatness" [39] or superiority: the qualities of moral virtue, we might say, that turn notable persons into heroes. Blameless, commonplace "goodness" seldom makes effective drama. Therefore the whole meaning of "goodness" affects the interpretations of what kind of person the tragic hero should be, and what effect he should create on the audience. Aristotle's tragic hero would be no goody-goody, unable, like many Neoclassical heroes of the Age of Reason, to depart from codes previously arranged for him; a man above temptation, a stranger to vulnerabilities. He would be a character of outstanding personality stationed, for greater conspicuousness, on the higher levels of social responsibility, somewhere between the extremes of good and bad, though inclining to good, and involved in tragedy by a human flaw of character or fatal error in judgment and conduct. Such a person, like humbler persons in ordinary life, may behave with "consistent inconsistency," [40] as all the greatest characters in fiction have behaved: a fact which Neoclassicists could not altogether appreciate because their interpretation of consistent character was limited and literal.

Luzán's own interpretation of Aristotle, inevitably erring on the side of bookish logic, led him back naturally to a general disapproval of Spanish plays and to an idea of "unity" of character, which, if not narrow in intention, was narrow in effect. As on several other important occasions, however, he chose to be guided about the character of the tragic hero by Corneille, whose understanding of the Aristotelian word "goodness" was more practical than academic. Corneille, let us remember, interpreting "goodness" as eminence, believed that Aristotle's text would admit of a protagonist with either a good or bad moral character, and that the term "goodness" must relate to poetic goodness—that is to say, artistic perfection in the delineation of any tragic personality.

In the circumstances, Luzán's choice of guide says much for his dispassionate judgment. It means that, despite his obsession with morals, he refused the temptingly didactic interpretation of Castelvetro who equated Aristotle's "goodness" with a Christian-like gentleness and meekness. It means that Don Ignacio, who often sought a compromise, discarded that of the relatively moderate Beni who suggested that the protagonist should simply be more virtuous than vicious. It is Corneille also to whom Luzán turns over the problem of consistency in character and methods of obtaining it. There were those who academically imagined that unity in character, as part of the Unity of Action, meant that dramatic persons must never change their opinions. But Corneille had asserted that a man may be inconstant by temperament, that a character's behavior at some crisis, or in some embarrassing situation, may be logically at variance with his inner feelings if only for the sake of keeping these hidden. Luzán must have recognized the realism of such arguments. At all events he agreed with Corneille that, to be constant, a character need not hold invariably to the same opinion, though at least he might be expected to adhere to the same general inclinations and not change his opinions unless presented with good reasons for doing so. Much therefore is conceded by Luzán to realistic psychology. At the same time we must not imagine that he had any true conception of the development of character—of those changes produced by maturing experience, or by the influence of one person's mind on another's that is the essence of mental reality and so of the drama closely imitating real life. All Classical theorists expected drama to imitate totalities and generalities, not individual susceptibilites and idiosyncracies. If Corneille himself could have considered it proper to imitate in drama the shifting, uncertain, irrational interests and influences operating in real life, he would have had to imitate by the help of his artistic instinct rather than by calculation.

It is significant that Luzán should give so much weight to characterization however static, psychologically speaking, his ideal characters might be. To deplore neglect of characterization, in the Spanish eighteenth century at least, was to criticize legitimately. Needless to say, he does not make the distinction which an English critic would make, or assume, between the value of psychological characterization for its own human sake, and the importance of selecting types who could be guaranteed to behave in character according to the manners of the milieu they represented. Luzán was not thinking of individuals such as were common in English drama and which often broke out of the poetic conventions of Spain's Golden Age. His objection to Golden Age "character" is largely to the flighty behavior of women types and braggart gallants liable, in his opinion, to corrupt morals, give the theater a bad name, and so unnecessarily provoke authorities to close the theaters down. His most realistic opinion on this subject is that important as "customs" are, they must not usurp the importance of action and plot. And in so far as Luzán, like Aristotle, was thinking of drama in its electrifying force, one must agree that a play devoted to the presentation of social manners and types alone is unlikely to exert dramatic force.

After surveying tragic style and diction, with renewed insistence on the appropriateness of language to speaker, Book III ends, somewhat summarily, with a review of nontragic genres. These are tragi-comedy; the *autos* already mentioned; the eclogues which, although arranged in reflective speeches, are more normally regarded as lyrical poetry; and pure comedy. Heroic dramas which admit of lighter interludes he dismisses as yet another breed of unnatural monsters, despite Corneille's support of them, and despite his own *Virtue Crowned*. If different dramatic *genres* are mixed, their moral message to the public would be ambiguous, he thought, and ambiguity in moral seriousness cannot be right.

[155]

Satire, to the surprise of some critics, is excluded altogether, and not, we think, unreasonably, since although its intention is different from that of inconsequential comedy, this difference is in degree rather than in kind. Had Luzán devoted as much space to all reaches and peculiarities of comedy as ideally he should have done, satire and farce would doubtless have figured as special sections. In the event comedy is treated as tragedy's poor relation, alike in physical structure but humbler in literary importance, and is relegated inadequately to the domesticity of ridiculing bourgeois vices. Never did Neoclassicists ask themselves the essential question, what is a sense of humor? Without Aristotelian prompting, the aesthetic theorists made a poor thing of aesthetic philosophy.

CHAPTER 10

The Poetics. *Book IV.*
The Grandeur of the Epic

WHEN Luzán in the company of other Preceptists legislated for the Epic, he seemed to envisage the possibility of an Epic future. In his judgment, apparently, the Epic was the highest form of poetic expression. For which reason he regretted that the genre had fallen out of use, or, at any rate, had fallen below acceptable standards,[1] and did not realize that the need for epic expression in society had been fulfilled by another form of art more in keeping with modern understanding: the novel.

Discussion of epic characteristics obliges Luzán to repeat himself considerably. The narrative form, the presentation of characters, the imitation of "life," the whole question of verisimilitude, the poet's purpose, the use of imagery, the unity of action, the relation of any one part to all the rest and to the beginning, middle, and end of the narrative . . . have all been discussed before in sections on lyrical and dramatic poetry, especially the latter. We shall, therefore, largely restrict our examination of Book IV to the best chapters of the Book—Chapter VII on the Epic hero, Chapter IX on the use of marvels as contributions to grandeur.

I *Definition of the Epic*

Aristotle had created difficulties for his disciples by failing to define the Epic as a genre. But Luzán, who had studied the commentators assiduously, knew that Aristotle's views on the subject might safely be deduced from his poetic principles in general. First he quotes the short definition commonly used by some interpreters as the gist of Aristotelian teaching on the subject: "Epic poetry is an imitation (that is, of nature or real life) obtained by means of narrative verse and of an action complete, sublime, and

[157]

distinct from ordinary history," [2] where the qualities of size and majesty on which Luzán devotes attention in ensuing chapters, are left unstressed. In fact, he prefers a much clumsier definition offered by Beni, presumably because, despite its verbosity, it covers all the qualities, including grandeur, which Luzán thought proper: "Epic poetry is the imitation of a sublime and illustrious action on a suitably grand scale, composed in heroic meter, by means of dramatic narrative, for the purpose of inspiring great wonder and pleasure and at the same time for the purpose of instructing those who direct and govern in matters concerning good customs and the living of a happy life, and with the idea of animating and stimulating such persons to the highest virtues and most noble deeds," [3] where nearly all the emphasis is placed on utility. However, for working purposes, this explanatory definition seemed to satisfy Luzán, and his chief interest was concentrated on elaborating it.

II Assessment of the Epic Hero and His Associates

In Chapter VII Luzán makes a deliberate and most valiant effort to investigate the inner reaches of the hero's "character." He does not quite achieve his aim. But he shows that he was aware of profundities which he could not fathom. The reason for his inability completely to satisfy himself or his reader is that his standards, like those of all Neoclassicists, had been taken from the models already set up: the stereotypes which inevitably provoked the stereotyped interpretation of Aristotle from which the Age of Reason in later decades would be trying to shake itself free. The only way in which a new Preceptist could develop his thinking on any aspect of character and characterization was to make from original observation the human analogies which already outside, and later inside, literature the epoch was preparing to authorize. One obvious way in which Luzán's contemporary, Feijoo, was able to develop any inherited thought was by testing it against his own human experience or against the human experiences accumulated for his personal judgment by history. This method could conduct any form of reason into original byways, if not original conclusions, and convert any series of particular items into universality.

Luzán, who directly and indirectly was influenced by Feijoo's practical thought and the climate of Spanish Enlightenment generally, was nevertheless not completely ready to venture very far on his own. His remarks on the possibilities of epic character, however intelligent and academically well informed, are based on prejudged archetypes. Nevertheless, he had given the subject considerable thought. He was not content merely to provide for the epic hero a naïve list of admirable qualities. He was interested in how such qualities would operate and, more significantly, why tradition presented him as it did—as we might say, why a hero is a hero. One of his preparatory observations in this respect is the suggestive statement that a man admires what is superior to himself: a fact of experience true for all time. Acknowledgment of superiority, then, ultimately explains the need for a recognizably great hero, and for the strong projection that his character must make.

Two other particular requirements, also true for all time, stand out in this chapter which otherwise is an expression of Luzán's thoughtful bafflement. One is that the superiority of the epic hero must relate convincingly to what the age for whom he is created understands by superiority. Which meant for Christian epochs, prompted Neoclassical reasoning, what the age understood by Christian ethics. The second related to a convention so firmly established that Luzán thought it would be idle—significantly he did not say it would be wrong—to resist traditional practice. This is the assumption that the epic hero is a man of outstanding physical valor.

Before we mentally criticize Luzán for tamely, since it would seem reluctantly, bowing to this convention at a time when scholars and artists were beginning to look affectionately for faults in great men and to accentuate the extraordinary importance of ordinary thoughts, words, and deeds, we should pause to take our modern bearings and search for modern analogies. Great epic poems have gone out of fashion. But we still think of "epic" actions in national experience, and represent them, in various ways, with contemporary fervor, through our own modern media. Often, nowadays, they relate to some large-scale, long-drawn-out national or multinational resistance to an invading enemy: a little country gathering its forces to withstand a giant, either in full-size war or in underground movements. Or they may relate to abnormally dangerous voyages of conquest into the unknown: the discovery of the American continent; the conquest of Granada, or Everest; the journey to the moon. The chief point to notice at these elevated, superphases of an "epic" hero's experience is that, while remaining verisimilar himself, he is temporarily living above his individual capacity, or perhaps is projected into all the fullness of potentiality which the state of emergency opens up to him. For the time being he is, as it were, another person, a universalized embodiment of willpower converted into physical activity or endeavor. Without this activity, so fundamental in Aristotelian theory for drama and Epic alike, there can be no Epic universally recognized as such. For activity of thinking, however powerful, is not of itself able to set fire to public imagination.

Physical prowess, therefore, or the conspicuous leader determining great physical activity, particularly in relation to abnormal battle areas, or abnormal distances, or heights, or depths, seems as essential to us in epic story as it did, despite any reluctance on his part, to Luzán. It must, seemingly, constitute an aspect of reality, and be, as he says, accepted. We may notice, too, on the same subject, that the "epic" hero at such a time loses his trivial accidentals and human weakness, probably in reality as well as in appearance. For awhile, at least, he has no leisure to live on an ordinary level, attend to ordinary needs, or respond to ordinary passions. Moreover, he is aware of the anxious eyes of his own men, or of his country, or of the world, critically upon him. Or, if he does act as a private person—like the Cid saying farewell to Jimena—these private concerns are seen as genuinely incidental to an overall, inspiring endeavor, and, in stirring times of crisis, by tacit consent, only the virtues of the leader's private life are normally noted. Further still, despite the fact that he is living on a plane superior to his normal self, he is not unconvincing to his onlookers. Emergency has made them partakers by will of what looks like his superhuman activity. Then even unbelievers tend to entertain religious, universal thoughts, for they are men alarmingly faced with inscrutable infinity and so outside themselves. Rarefied moments of this kind have therefore been part of the experience of nearly all peoples in nearly all centuries, and collectively acquire conventional attributes. The traditional epic hero may be archetypal. But archetypes can be permanently realistic. The artist's business is, in one medium or another, to relate his epic hero to the universal experience of momentousness.

For the most part, however, Chapter VII reflects Luzán's struggle, which is the struggle of all intelligent Neoclassicists, to apprehend something above and beyond the conventional qualities of epic heroes—their courage, moral rectitude, and so on: something that is not just the effect of a sum total of their virtues, but which makes each great hero different from every other great hero in life or literature; something which makes the noble, valorous Aeneas, Luzán says, different from the noble, valorous Achilles. We suggest that the word which eluded him and his colleagues, even had they known it in its modern applications, is *personality*. Aristotle and other ancient theorists had not been explicit about it. But a much nearer authority had supplied the idea to Luzán's Spain. Feijoo's polemical work, well known since the first publication of the first volume of his *Universal Theater of Criticism* in 1726, had been absorbed by all the Spanish intellectuals of his time and influenced them with or without their knowledge, with or without their volition. The title of a stimulating essay on the unknown quantity in life and genius called "I Know Not What" was published in Volume VI of the *Theater* in 1734.[4] A new version of its title might well be "The Unknown Quantity in Human and Stylistic Personality" in recognition of that unknown factor sought almost with enthrallment by the humanly orientated eighteenth century.

The collective good and bad qualities which, says Luzán, distinguish each epic hero, go to form "what Italians and French call *character*, a word to which I have been obliged to resort because our own words like *temperament (genio), inclinations, habits, disposition (natural)*, do not adequately or appropriately express the idea. For *character* is what especially belongs to one person and not to anybody else." [5] Very likely it was Luzán's Italian schooling which was preventing him from seeking good Spanish words. The inventive Spaniards can always find suitable equivalents for foreign terms if they care to make the effort. And Feijoo had already made a much better business of the problem, despite his puzzle-title "I Know Not What." Luzán's words at one point almost paraphrase those of his senior:

". . . just as the arrangement of the features which give beauty to a face would, if transferred to another (type of) face, disfigure it, because those features belong exclusively to the original and are placed in suitable proportion and measurement, so, what for one character looks right, in another would seem disproportionate." [6]

The trouble, Luzán found, was that this uniqueness must, for epic purposes, be given superlative significance. Also, since it was not to consist of a mere bundle of perfections, it must show degree as well as kind. Without being able to say so, in so many words, he clearly realized that the unknown quantity must be a complex unit and the riddle of its essential complexity he could not quite resolve.

No Neoclassicist had managed to discover the secret of master-personality either in real or fictitious heroes. But many Neoclassicists had taken part in a search for it. Luzán represents the best results of their inquiry when he talks about our need to admire someone superior to ourselves. For surely epic personality has a good deal to do with tantalizing strength in incalculable reserve, therefore a superiority mysteriously shrouded, or just out of reach; with an anticipated nobility of thought and competence displayed in an endless variety of disconcertingly unexpected ways as if from an infinitude of resources; with the ability to seize the initiative, especially against great odds, and therefore to dominate a dangerous occasion. All this in epic poetry must of course be more consistently and successfully demonstrated than in life, and where a morally good hero is portrayed, any of the trivial defects which all individuals possess will generally, one must admit, detract from the force of his superlative effort.

Realistic, too, from the human as well as from the aesthetic point of view, is Don Ignacio's comment, in a gloss of Le Bossu, that for epic purposes one of the hero's admirable qualities should be allowed to predominate. It would presumably be the one, like boldness, or steadfastness, or epic patience, most urgently called out by necessity. Luzán's willingness to follow the epic convention of using some military or physically momentous theme as the material of epic poetry is closely related to the same realistic experience. Epics possibly may be derived from peaceful subjects. But it is danger which most obviously releases a great man's potential from the bonds of the trivially actual, and it is danger which unites peoples into effort on the largest, and possibly noblest scale.

Where Luzán and various other eighteenth-century theorists differ fundamentally from critics of other centuries is over the academic education of the epic poet. As stated in Chapter VII, he should be a profoundly learned scholar with specialization in Moral Philosophy: a discipline from which Don Ignacio expects him to acquire the profound wisdom necessary to his task. Modern critics would not care to demand more than general culture—if that—as a basis for creative writing. But the eighteenth century had a more innocent faith than has the twentieth in the supreme importance of booklearning for the teaching of wisdom and rectitude. On the other hand, Luzán now shakes himself free from the narrowly pious belief of many of his contemporaries throughout Europe that the public should be protected from acquaintance with characters who are morally bad. He insists, as he had insisted at the beginning of the *Poetics,* that morally bad characters are only "bad" for public morals if they get away with their badness scot free. To us this may not seem a very important argument. To the eighteenth century, in which controversy over the moral lawfulness of presenting drama at all, of keeping play-houses open at all, still resounded, it was a major concession, especially from a man with important Church connections.

Yet if the villain was to receive his poetic dues, it was right, thought Luzán, that the convention by which the epic hero also received the just reward of his labors should be respected as well. Aristotle and Horace had failed to pronounce on the matter, and Neoclassicists were inclined to judge from epic practice. If Luzán had known the *Chanson de Roland,* he might not have called it an epic poem. Defeat to his captious century could hardly amount to epic grandeur, even if Charlemagne lived to fight another day. However, the disaster at Roncevaux was a national disaster acceptable as a mournful incident set in a glorious saga. Where the full history is known, incidental tragedies are not seen in isolation and the *Chanson de Roland* in consequence would not break with epic tradition. The story of remoter, half-legendary peoples is more self-contained. A long struggle about unknown or little-known peoples, ending in final disaster, would be likely to have an effect not morally encouraging, but depressive. Thus Luzán was probably right to ask for a happy end to the hero's adventures.

III   *Rulings on the Supernatural*

Finally, a further chapter to offer special evidence of Luzán's scholarly common sense is Chapter IX on epic marvels, supernatural machines, and deities. Patently Luzán enjoyed the pictorial world of mythology and the marvels and wonders that inflame poets' imaginations and color descriptive passages. But, like all men of good taste, he was offended by the incongruity of marvels too obviously contrived, used for their own sensational sake or the narrator's mere convenience. Eighteenth-century scholars were acutely aware of what Feijoo had been saying about wonders and marvels in real life, and even aesthetic critics now touched the subject of marvels somewhat gingerly, almost apologetically. Luzán, earlier, in Chapter IV, concerned with epic themes and plots, had closely followed one of Feijoo's most publicized arguments: that "it is very common and very natural for those who relate some strange, unusual happening, always to add something to fill the story out in order to occasion more wonder and more interest," [7] and he had used the argument to stress the importance of proportion and good sense.

Now, in the circumstances of the Epic, wonders and marvels would not be a disadvantage, so long, Luzán warns still in the interests of reason, so long as they are used judiciously. The sense of proportion to be observed in legitimate artistic contexts where gods speak, oracles prophesy, and nonhuman beings assert themselves, is to be exercised largely, according to Chapter IX, to prevent supernatural phenomena from acquiring more than incidental importance. For instance, Luzán objects to angels who take upon themselves the exclusive responsibility of winning the hero's battle for him, or to gods who provide miracle solutions to save the poet trouble.

The most important comment made in this connection, however, is in disagreement with Boileau.[8] As we heard in his remarks on the pagan subject matter of modern tragedy, Luzán believed from the exercise of his personal common sense, that if modern poets engaged supernatural assistance, they ought to do so through the kind of supernatural agency familiar to modern understanding: that is to say, miracles, dreams, visions, or apparitions employed not by pagans, but by Christians. In his considered opinion, the Christian world of miracle and marvel could supply all the imaginative suggestion and inspiration required, though he was not so literal or carping a critic that he could object to well-known figures of speech taken from Classical mythology to serve purely as decoration. Nevertheless, he seems to have had strong feelings against the case for pagan subject matter, not so much on religious grounds as on those of anachronism and incongruity. He added to his notes for the second edition a further protest, giving as an example of what he disliked the introduction of mythological characters into Luis de Camoens' *Os Lusíadas (Portugal's Story of Renown)* which he otherwise revered. Probably by 1754 he had read more of Milton's *Paradise Lost* with the spiritual realism of which the *Lusíadas* compares unfavorably.

In any case, Classical mythology, like Baroque images, had become trite by Luzán's time. His persistent demand that diction, decoration, and all the rest of poetic mystique should be unequivocally up-to-date in new compositions places him among those enlightened and by no means unimaginative rationalists of whom Feijoo was the conspicuous leader. Whatever form Spain's literature was destined to take, that literature could not thrive on ideas belonging to the past. Which, perhaps, is the most penetrating idea in the whole of Luzán's message.

CHAPTER 11

Reception of the Poetics

"All that this work lacks, is readers" [1]

DON Ignacio may have expected, may possibly have hoped, that his reformist *Poetics* would provoke a storm of opposition somewhat similar to the storm which in a different quarter of Enlightenment Feijoo had been provoking deliberately and effectively by his *Universal Theater of Criticism*. It looks very much as if Luzán had borrowed the challenging tone of his opening chapters from the Benedictine scholar he so greatly admired; as if, too, he was convinced, like other Enlightened Spaniards, that the reformer's first act should be to shake the nation's complacency. Nor could he have failed to observe that, by the violence of their attacks, most of Feijoo's prejudiced opponents were making themselves public laughing stocks. Sarcastic laughter is an incisive weapon. The Aragonese, however, unlike Professor Feijoo whose aims were entirely practical, was interested in debate for its own intellectual sake. His tone academically is set for academic argument. Not for him were the human doubts which sometimes made Feijoo disagree with himself and say so in print. Luzán assumes that his own reasoning is sound because it is based on sound precedents judged to be sound by sound modern authorities. He did not ask himself, as Feijoo might have done, "What do I mean by *sound?*" and "Are there more kinds of *soundness* than the one I know?" In fact, opposition to the *Poetics* was not slow to appear. But most of the Spanish controversy over Neoclassical principles swirled around books which, whether influenced by the *Poetics* or not, were rather more colorful. Hence Luzán's work tended to be regarded as a Neoclassical *vade mecum* rather than as a direct instrument of polemic, and was not even noticed outside Spain until Luzán himself, on his official business in France, became physically visible.

Most of Don Ignacio's provocative remarks, therefore, were

best known to the fully converted, or to those admirers of Golden Age achievement who realized in all fairness that the eighteenth century too had a peculiar literary message to convey in its own peculiar manner, and that Luzán's promotion of law and order was a necessary means of making the overdue dramatic change from lyrical emotion to human matter-of-factness. It would be from among this latter group especially that the most unexpected and unwelcome criticisms of the *Poetics* would come. For instance, inherent in the official Approbations of the 1737 edition are mixed feelings: admiration, certainly, of Luzán's revival and his Spanish codification of ancient laws of poetic orderliness; yet unease at the Preceptist's tendency to pursue his logic to unpractical, and hence unacceptable, extremes.

Writers of Approbations were usually distinguished scholars and ecclesiastics who acted as censor-readers of any given book and academic sponsors of its published appearance. The two gentlemen sponsoring the 1737 *Poetics* may be counted among Luzán's admirers. Dr. Miguel Navarro, a theologian of the University of Zaragoza, Luzán's home town, is impressed both by the authoritative nature of the work and by Luzán's own erudition. He is willing to believe that Spanish dramatists of the Golden Age, for all the brilliance of their personal inspiration, would have been greater than ever if they could have adjusted themselves to Aristotelian rules. But even this prejudiced cleric cannot help but remark that some of Luzán's censures of Spanish dramatists may be mistaken. His treatment of the Spanish theater would always detract from Luzán's prestige in Spain. Here, from the very beginning, honest Spanish Neoclassicists were obliged to part company with him over some of his basic suppositions. Here, probably, was one reason why his work "lacked readers."

Speaking along exactly the same lines, his cosponsor, Father Gallinero, of the Order of Preachers, was much more forthright. He, too, believed that all the Arts need their rules. He, too, thought that Lope de Vega condescended over much to the masses and might be said to have laid himself open to blame for doing so. But he roundly condemned any foreign sneering as "utterly intolerable." Father Gallinero was not, it seems, a man to be gulled by mere words. Within the very cover of the *Poetics*, almost in the spiritual presence of Aristotle himself, he could declare without courtesy of qualification, that if Spanish Golden

Age playwrights departed from the Preceptists the explanation lay not in Spanish inadequacy but in Spanish superiority. For drama, in Aristotle's time, Father Gallinero explained, had not yet reached its peak of perfection. More, he went on, anticipating Luzán's strictures of Spanish "defects," any "defects" revealed by Spanish dramatists are equaled by other kinds of defects in dramas of other nations: of France, for example. With immense satisfaction, he quoted, for France's benefit, the protest of one of her greatest dramatists, Molière, that critics treat Rules as if Rules are the "greatest mysteries on earth," whereas they are nothing more than "convenient observations"; [2] to which he further added Molière's suggestion, so reminiscent of a remark by Lope de Vega, that probably the greatest rule of all is to give satisfaction.[3] Remembering a little belatedly at this point, however, that he was sponsoring a Neoclassical work, Father Gallinero hastened to assure the reader that Don Ignacio blended praise of Golden Age writers with his blame, and that his discreet reference to Spanish faults had been calculated to steal the foreigners' thunder. Handsomely, therefore, Luzán is given the benefit of this doubt, though, as the whole tone of the *Poetics* shows, Don Ignacio's mention of Spanish virtues was less from conviction than from necessary self-defense.

I *Journal of the Spanish Men of Letters*

In Luzán's day the only truly learned Spanish journal was the short-lived *Diario de los literatos de España (Journal of the Spanish Men of Letters)*, a worthy counterpart of its French model *Journal des Savants (The Savants' Journal)*, and published between 1737 and 1742. Spanish Enlightenment was not yet sufficiently developed to support the objectivity of a literary journal of this calibre. But during its short life, the *Journal* duly recorded and assessed with fairness and objectivity the few learned works of the period worthy of permanent notice. Luzán's *Poetics* stands in this respect in the most illustrious company available, and its mere presence, in Volume IV of the *Journal*, would have commended it to the interest of posterity.

For this reason too, it is most significant that the *Journal* in its general assessment of the *Poetics* should come to the same conclusions as Dr. Navarro, Father Gallinero, and nearly all dispassionate friends and critics of Don Ignacio's work. Approval of the *Poetics'* search for order, proportion, and verisimilitude is unstinted. The *Journal* is proud to think that Spain can produce so worthy an equivalent to foreign codes of aesthetics, and it likes Luzán's well-reasoned commentaries on the history and essence of Poetry and his explanation of Neoclassical ideals. To this extent the *Journal* obviously saw Luzán as a champion of Spain's honor: a view of him potentially impressive to Spanish patriots in times when decadent Spain was sensitive to the self-confident criticism of ascendant France, and while she was temporarily too weak to answer back.

Accordingly much space is devoted by the *Journal* to the historical value of the *Poetics,* and also to the suitability for modern times of Neoclassical techniques. So enthusiastic is the reviewer about these subjects that he expends considerable energy on a lengthy summary of the contents. Wherefore, since any cultured Spanish reader of current publications would be familiar with the *Journal* whose miscellaneous articles appealed to a larger public than did the *Poetics,* it may be suspected that much of the century's knowledge about the *Poetics* itself, knowledge strangely vague and limited, would be derived from the *Journal's* conveniently simplified summary rather than from the original.

Once again, however, Luzán's admirers draw the line of their approbation precisely at that point where he applies his Neoclassical yardstick to Golden Age mastery. But the sober *Journal* surprises us by a warm defense not only of Golden Age dramatists, not only of Lope de Vega specifically, but of Luis de Góngora, whose mazelike *Soledades (Solitudes)* seemed to many fair-minded critics of the rational eighteenth century impossible to justify. Even critics not altogether averse to the sensuous luxuriance of Góngora's Baroque contortions sometimes sacrificed him to foreign displeasure. Least of all, therefore, should we expect admirers of Luzán, and all Luzán stood for, to range themselves so committedly behind Góngora as did the *Journal of the Spanish Men of Letters.*

First, in response to Luzán's "severe and rather impassioned"[4] judgments of Golden Age dramatists, the *Journal* bases its defense of Lope on the argument, now unconvincing but then credible, that Lope, by his own account in his *New Art of Writing Plays (Arte nuevo de hacer comedias),* broke the laws to please his public. Certainly this was a way of placing the irresistible Lope beyond criticism and of transferring blame to the tyrannical masses. Yet, despite the convenience of such an argument, the *Journal* is later only too eager to dispute, as Lope had disputed in theory and practice, the Neoclassical opinion that a mixture of seriousness and comedy is unlifelike, and denies that tragi-comedy is the "monster" that Luzán called it, or that it was unknown to the Ancients. The reviewer also disagrees with Neoclassicists' contentions that comedy in a serious drama is distracting. Equally distracting in that case, declares the *Journal*, is the tender love scene. Most interesting of all, however, in this context are the *Journal's* words describing Lope's manner in his *New Art* . . . , a manner which the majority of eighteenth-century critics completely overlooked. The *New Art* . . . , we recall, was to be read by invitation before the Academy of Madrid, a body that was perfectly well aware of how Lope's *Art* worked in practice. There, honored by august admirers, was a brilliant dramatist who knew that they knew that he knew exactly how brilliant he was. The *Journal*, which had spoken of Lope's very correct attitude to the Ancients in theory, uses to describe his manner the words "the elegant dash and spirited ingenuity with which he handled an academic subject," [5] a description which captures Lope's tone of occasion completely. How often a modern writer, invited to address an academic audience on some auspicious occasion, smilingly adopts the tone: "I can't vouch for the—let us say—historical accuracy of my portrait of this historical character. I'm afraid I ignore the historians. I'm a working playwright and don't write for you scholars." But when the modern artist speaks in such a way, on such an occasion, he is not deprecating his own capricious art. Neither does he expect his hearers to deprecate it. On the contrary, as an artist, he is amiably talking down to the scholars, as, on scholarly subjects, he would expect them amiably to talk down to him. Lope surely was observing a genial convention which Luzán, the *Journal*, and many of Lope's own apologists of the eighteenth century took too seriously. Artists do not measure their words as scholars are obliged to do. So the *Journal*, to our mind, offers, despite itself, the best evidence of all by referring to Lope's tone. It was not his admission of guilt that mattered, but the cheerful tone, indicative of mutual condescension, in which he confessed that "guilt."

On the subject of Góngora, the *Journal* shows a strange advance on eighteenth-century literalness. For it was able to distinguish between extravagance which is artistic and literary, and extravagance which is merely decadent, like, we may say, that of Góngora's eighteenth-century imitators who copied from his art only its most obvious externals. Astonishingly, for an admirer of the new Classicism, the *Journal*, without denying certain faults in Góngora, defends some of his extreme metaphors which Luzán had condemned. One of them was the "sepulchres of foam," [6] denounced by Luzán for its obscurity; though any unprejudiced interpreter, argued the *Journal*, again hitting the nail on the head by this descriptive adjective, could perfectly well understand what Góngora's phrase meant in its proper context.

The *Journal's* word "unprejudiced" [7] was in fact the key word to any of its advice on the subject of literary criticism. When Luzán was dealing with Classical and Neoclassical literature, he was usually fair-minded, often acute. But, in spite of his patronizing praise, from time to time, of the good qualities of Golden Age writers—praise often more offensive in tone than his blame—he was not a dispassionate critic of non-Classical literature, and, given his circumstances, could hardly be expected to appreciate non-Classical works of art. In the end the *Journal* comes to the conclusion later reached by the wisest of eighteenth-century critics, Neoclassical or otherwise, that many of the Rules established by Preceptists, however helpful, represent merely the particular taste of a particular period or nation.[8]

II *On the Margin of Polemic*

Strenuous, though by no means organized, polemic over the validity of Neoclassical principles which broke out in midcentury and spread, with shifting attitudes on both Neoclassical and Nationalist sides, across later decades, was not a direct result of Luzán's theorizing. It was provoked by certain practical demonstrations on the part of writers who shared Luzán's reformist views, who used his *Poetics* for reference, and who sometimes quoted him.

Perhaps if Luzán had never copied the French and Italian habit of attacking Spanish masterpieces, his friends and admirers would also have left the past alone and both the *Poetics* and Neoclassical doctrine generally would not have been regarded with suspicion. But in that case the eighteenth century would have been critically and analytically the poorer. For the supreme importance of the apparently senseless controversy was that it helped Spanish critics to clear their minds and eventually to learn in literature, as they were learning from other experiences, political, philosophical, social, and scientific, that truth could no longer be described in simple, dogmatic terms. Quite as sane and sound, academically speaking, as criticism from trained and wholehearted Neoclassicists is the criticism of Luzán by Porcel in the Academy of Good Taste, of Nasarre by Tomás de Zavaleta, and of the antinational periodical *El Pensador (The Thinker)* and Nicolás de Moratín by Nipho.[9] It was from jaded familiarity with such confrontations that critics of the 'eighties and 'nineties began to value temperateness. Luzán himself shows that he, too, was capable of development. Had he still been alive in the second half of the century he would not, we think, have sided with Neoclassical extremists.

One sure means of achieving international distinction in the first half of the eighteenth century was to be noticed by the learned French journal *Memoranda . . . . . for the History of Science and Letters* published by the Jesuits of Trévoux.[10] This journal had as yet taken little account of Spain in decadence. It was extremely ill-informed on Peninsular affairs and had seen no occasion to inform itself better. Vaguely, foreign critics assumed that Spain for the time being had little or nothing of value to offer the rest of Europe. Little indeed had been accomplished in Spanish literature since 1700. But some of Feijoo's books had appeared, were duly reviewed in the foreign press, and were translated into French from 1742 onwards. A few other scholarly works had also been published. And Luzán's *Poetics,* one might have supposed, would have attracted the attention of French critics interested in decrying Spanish dramatic taste and preaching reform on the French pattern.

Certain Spanish scholars, Luzán among them, had become aware of this curious gap in the *Memoranda's* international knowledge, and were affronted above all by a letter printed in the French journal in March, 1742, which remarked on France's small literary commerce with Spain and on the tendency to believe that there was little in Spanish Letters calling for notice by international scholars. From Don Juan's report on his father's activities, we learn that Luzán had shouldered the task of answering the *Memoranda* in a public Latin Letter, *Epistola,* to be published, it was hoped, in Madrid. The preparation of this Apology for Spanish eighteenth-century achievement, however, was delayed, so Don Juan tells us, and the *Epistola* was eventually published in Zaragoza in 1743, together with letters explaining why it had not appeared earlier.[11] A fuller explanation of the postponement is given in the Zaragoza document itself which informs us that the distinguished scholars, invited to express their opinions on the *Epistola,* doubted the value of those Spanish authors whom Luzán wanted to parade for the *Memoranda's* benefit, and thought that his gesture would not be fully approved in Spain.

The Zaragoza document of 1743 exists in the National Library of Spain and corresponds to the details given by Don Juan.[12] The name on the title page is an assumed one, "Ignacio Philalethes." But the work is catalogued under the pseudonym "Lanuza," which Luzán is also known to have used. It consists of three separate letters. One of them, the original *Epistola* directed to the *Memoranda*—written in Latin, presumably for its greater circulation abroad, Latin still being the academic language—objects to the *Memoranda's* cavalier dismissal of Spain's intellectual activity in the eighteenth century, mentions the establishment of various Spanish Academies of the period, and, among modern Spanish writers worthy of notice, instances Nasarre, Feijoo, Martín Sarmiento, Francisco Huerta, and Montiano. Luzán's own name is strikingly conspicuous by its modest absence.[13]

More interesting for our purposes than the *Epistola* itself are the Preface and the two attendant Letters in Spanish. The Preface identifies the document for us as the one mentioned by Don Juan. "Ignacio Philalethes," expressing his concern about the *Memoranda's* attitude, describes the author of the *Epistola*—that is, himself—as an Aragonese, who, in 1742, had been staying in Madrid, and who, on return to Aragon, had written an *Epistola* addressed to the Editors of the *Memoranda,* and had sent this *Epistola* for the approval of several erudite friends. It is then that he gives the reason for delay in publication. Over a year transpired, he says, before his manuscript was returned to him by the friend for whose advice he had applied; and when it came, it was accompanied by a letter from the said friend doubting the

Epistola's choice of Spanish authors. The "friend's" Letter is included in the 1743 set. Still more important is a third Letter included under the title of *The Author's Reply to the Foregoing Letter*, that is, the Reply of the author of the original *Epistola* to his "friend's" comments on it.

Here, after some preliminary courtesies, "Ignacio Philalethes" speaks of his friend's reasons for wanting to suppress the *Epistola:* one reason, the choice of Spanish authors, and the other reason, a fear of displeasing a nation—meaning France— which "today distributes alms to the Spanish muses." [14] This infers that the Francophile *friend* had not been anxious to suggest to the distinguished French *Memoranda* that it was being held up to Spanish criticism.

"Ignacio Philalethes" protests that his intention had been in no way discourteous; that he has no prejudice against foreigners— a fact patently true—and that a fair-minded Frenchman might be expected to agree that not even French authors are perfect. The message of his *Epistola,* "Ignacio Philalethes" explains, is that French critics, presumably aware that artistic defects are not peculiar to Spaniards but are found in all literatures, ought to exercise more Christian charity towards their neighbors; and that if foreign journals are to be intent on looking for nothing but defects in Spanish works, it might be more sensible for them not to review Spanish works at all. French critics of the Peninsula do not know their Spain, says "Ignacio Philalethes," a little belligerent now in the remoteness of his anonymity.

Significantly, one of the typical French arguments taken up is that eighteenth-century Spanish scholars are mere copyists. "Ignacio Philalethes" evidently remembered that Feijoo ignorantly had been criticized for "copying." Accordingly he points, with scholarly truth, to the fact that "copying" can be of two kinds, good and bad, and that in one way or another, every scholar is dependent on somebody else. Feijoo and Sarmiento, for instance, he insists, are copyists in the good sense. By which he evidently understood that they availed themselves of the new ideas of modern scholars for the purpose of discussing them, analyzing them, and assessing them. Indeed, largely of such stuff must all scholarship be made. Of such, at all events, was French scholarship in the eighteenth century.

But Ignacio Philalethes's most revealing remarks are those

which he applies to himself. For this disguised "Aragonese" had been a most assiduous "copyist," and he now defends himself from the possible interpretation of "copying" as plagiarizing:

"Even I, in what I have produced so far, do not consider that I have been a copyist in the bad and servile sense, for although, on the one hand, it is not seemly for me to speak well and enthusiastically of my own works—such being an offense against modesty—at the same time to despise them and disparage them more than is just would be an offense against sincerity": [15] a sane point sanely expressed.

Rightly he would be thinking, in all "sincerity," of the standards of his own critical *Poetics,* and of the *Journal of the Spanish Men of Letters,* for, "as for me," he goes on to his *friend,* "you know very well that one of the tendencies for which I have been reprehended by my learned censors is that I have been very rigid in my criticism and have held ideas about poetry which were too philosophical." [16] It must have been very hard for the modest and Classically-minded Luzán, who eventually with less than justice was to be placed on the level of Boileau by the *Memoranda* itself, not merely to have been ignored, but never yet to have been brought to the notice of those French Classicists who professed in 1742 to have made a Spanish survey and found so little worth report.

Some years later the *Memoranda* was to pay deferential tribute to Luzán, but that was not until 1748 when Don Ignacio, by then an important personage in ambassadorial circles, was meeting French savants personally and was becoming known as a distinguished visitor with first-hand information to give about Peninsular resurgence. The year 1748, significantly too, was the year after the *Memoranda* had at last discovered the *Journal of the Spanish Men of Letters* containing a long summary and approving review of the *Poetics.* Moreover, any disagreement by the *Memoranda* with Luzán's findings is couched in courtly terms of respect due to a distinguished foreigner personally known to France. Nevertheless, the *Memoranda's* articles, on the whole, still indicate that French critics knew remarkably little about Spanish Letters, and the French journal, in its ignorance, helped to pinpoint those sections of Luzán's *Poetics* which were least suitable for emphasis.

The *Memoranda* devotes considerable space in May, June, and

July of 1748 to an analysis of the *Poetics*. In general it makes much of the idea, which might more appropriately have been overlooked, that Luzán was acting in the interests of Spanish honor by at last proclaiming the Rules of Art. It is impressed with the profundity of his reading. Though it notices his lack of English scholarship, surmising that either Luzán had read no English works or that he did not approve of English literary idiosyncrasies. And it is in this context of English misdemeanor and French and Luzanesque rectitude that the *Memoranda* regrets French neglect of the Spanish language, of the study of the *Poetics* especially, since "all that this work lacks is readers."

More knowledgeably, the *Memoranda* gently corrected Luzán's misinterpretation of Horace's word *dulcia*, as *dulce*, sweet,[17] and courteously implied that Luzán in translating the word must nevertheless have had, at the back of his mind, the sense of *attractive* rather than sweet. Doubtless the *Memoranda* knew very well that Luzán had at the back of his mind nothing of the sort, as his examples make very clear. Also the *Memoranda* regretted (July, 1748) that Spanish printers had done less than justice to Don Ignacio by being unable to provide Greek lettering for his Greek words; a fault which the editors of the 1789 version attempted to right. In June the *Memoranda* stressed the didactic value of Preceptists to their respective nations, and smugly remarked that if France and Italy had shown an advance on other nations, that was because these countries had had the advantage of more instructors. It is curious to think of the didactic *Memoranda,* situated there between England and Spain, and making friends with the Italianized Luzán over supposed iniquities of Elizabethan and Spanish Golden Age masters. It is curious, because those two unprofessional nations, superficially so unlike, often look curiously similar when attacked by a third party. Particularly they sometimes seem startlingly alike in their amused refusal to take a Preceptist at his own valuation. The *Memoranda* evidently felt very strongly on the matter of English unwillingness to adopt French standards. It brought up the subject again in July when it regretted that the "republican" spirit of poetic England "always confused liberty with licence"—words undoubtedly borrowed from Milton [18] whom the *Memoranda* liked in spite of itself, but whose "licence" the *Memoranda* compared with the literary arrogance *(fierté)* of Golden Age Spain. Like Luzán, the

Memoranda was shocked, for example, by the "licence" of mixing or juxtaposing seriousness with comedy. So Luzán is praised for bravely underlining Spanish defects, and the *Memoranda* ends its reasoned eulogy of the *Poetics* with congratulations to Spain for producing such a patriotic work. Don Ignacio must have felt well rewarded for his venture.

This was not the end of the *Memoranda's* interest in Luzán. Once apprised of his principles, and his example, so it thought, to a degenerate Spain, it made the most of him. He is mentioned graciously again in May, 1750, as a contributor to Spanish culture, and in the December of the same year, when the *Memoranda* heard of the Discourses and plays of Montiano, a reviewer, inaccurately though naturally, attributed Montiano's work to the influence of Luzán, though Montiano, in fact, was not a disciple but a colleague. It was now that the *Memoranda* described Luzán as the Spanish equivalent of Boileau. And indeed on this occasion the French journal knew what it was saying and spoke truly, even doing Luzán scant justice. Finally, in January, 1752, the *Memoranda* reviewed Luzán's translation *Reason Versus Convention* from La Chaussée's *The Man of Modish Taboos* in the terms we have already discussed.[19]

It was not Luzán's destiny to be given much publicity again. But recently academic interest in him has revived to a certain extent. Both Dr. J. Cano and Dr. R. P. Sebold,[20] for instance, have done him the justice of assuming that he is at least as worthy of a scholar's notice as the Boileau with whom the *Memoranda* compared him. Of course Luzán's name was bandied about in the controversies of the eighteenth and nineteenth centuries, but not with any objective understanding of the details of the *Poetics*. For the most part he was a name normally associated with condemnation of Golden Age masters, and so a name used all too vaguely in partisan debate. The blame for such a state of affairs must ultimately and unhappily be ascribed to Luzán himself. Yet it is ironical to think that blame must be referred to the rather over-confident and still half-informed scholar of 1737. We believe that an older Luzán, somewhat older than he was when he died, would have learned to appreciate better the ultimate significance of the course he was following instinctively. In all probability, he would have looked back less and would have looked forward constructively towards modern rationalism. He should have been regarded as a highly cultured scholar in the philosophical area, a guide to an interpretation of the Classics, and, like the new Academy of the Spanish Language, a standard for correct literary speech and a model for empirical reasoning.

Still, it is no small honor to be called a Spanish Boileau by a distinguished French journal prejudiced against Spain and taught by Boileau himself to belittle Spanish genius. Therefore, despite his potentialities for surpassing Boileau, we may be well content to leave Luzán where in 1752 the *Memoranda* left him, enfolded in the security of French approbation.

Notes and References

Chapter One

1. The original version, from which our account is taken, exists in manuscript in the Biblioteca Nacional, Madrid. It was reproduced, with the exception of a few minor details, as preface to the second edition of the *Poética* in 1789, and as an introduction to Luzán's poems in *Biblioteca de Autores Españoles* (Madrid, Rivadeneira, 1952), LXI, 95–105. For the reader's convenience, our page references are to this later published version. The manuscript title is *Vida de Don Ignacio de Luzán (Life of Don Ignacio de Luzán)*. It is in two parts: a biography and an assessment of Luzán's talent and achievement. The printed version of 1789 and those taken from it omit some of the details of Luzán's minor achievements.

2. The Biblioteca Nacional, Madrid, possesses a series of somewhat tense letters which, from 1780 to 1789, passed between Don Juan Ignacio de Luzán, then a Canon of the Cathedral of Segovia, and various persons concerned with the publication of the second edition of the *Poética*. From these we learn of the health problems of Don Juan and the frustrations of all the parties concerned in collecting, organizing, and agreeing upon the material for the final form. Don Juan's malady had mental symptoms of acute depression. He died shortly after writing his final letter to Eugenio de Llaguno y Amírola in June of 1789. See Llaguno's note attached to the manuscript collection of these letters.

3. *Biblioteca de Autores Españoles*, hereinafter *BAE, ed. cit.*, pp. 95–96.

4. See *Historia general de España* (Toledo: Rodríguez, 1601), 2 vols. Later editions were enlarged.

5. *BAE*, p. 97.

6. *Ibid.*, p. 96.

7. *Ibid.*, p. 97.

8. Don Juan thinks that an academic or religious career may have been in his father's mind originally. See *op. cit.*, p. 9.

9. *Op. cit.*, p. 97.

10. *Ibid.*

11. *Ibid.*
12. *Ibid.* p. 98.
13. *Ibid.*
14. *Ibid.*
15. See pp. 77 ff., and note 11 to Chapter 5 below.

Chapter Two

1. The Minutes *(Actas)* of the Academy of Good Taste exist in manuscript in the Biblioteca Nacional, No. 18476–1–26. They consist of a series of records of attendance, of the members' contributions, and of certain other details, together with a collection of the members' poems and criticism. The pages are loose, unnumbered, and presumably incomplete.

2. The Marchioness of Sarria is described in the contemporary French learned journal, *Mémoires pour l'Histoire des Sciences et des Beaux Arts,* Trévoux, (Jan., 1752, p. 92) as the sister-in-law of the Count of Carvajal, "Minister of State," and as a lover and patroness of Letters. The Marquis of Sarria was her second husband. See L. A. de Cueto, Marqués de Valmar: *Bosquejo histórico—crítico de la poesía castellana en el siglo XVIII, BAE,* No. 61 (Madrid: Rivadeneira, 1952) pp. LXXXIX ff.

3. Outstanding persons have been identified by L. A. de Cueto, the Marqués de Valmar, on a sheet attached to the manuscript. They include Nasarre, Montiano, J. Porcel, L. J. Velázquez, etc. Others disguised as El Remiso (The Remiss One), El Aburrido (The Bored One) etc., are not recognizable.

4. See *Actas,* July 16th and August 20th, 1750.

5. See M. Menéndez y Pelayo: *Historia de las ideas estéticas en España,* V (Madrid: Editorial Hernanda, 1923), 235.

6. *Comedias y Entremeses de Miguel de Cervantes Saavedra,* 2 vols. (Madrid: Marín, 1749).

7. He is the author of two tragedies, *Virginia* (Madrid: Mercurio, 1750) and *Ataulpho* (Madrid: Mercurio, 1753). They are accompanied by critical discourses on dramatic theory.

8. See *Actas,* No. XII. It is a note in pencil on this prose discourse that assigns it to Velázquez.

9. See Ludovico Antonio Muratori: *Della perfetta poesia italiana* . . . in *Opere,* Vol. I, in the series: *La Letteratura Italiana,* Ed. R. Mattioli, etc., XLIV (Milan-Naples: Ricardo Ricciardi, undated), 59–176. See pp. 93 ff.

10. See *Cartas eruditas (Intellectual Letters)* II, 6. Clásicos Castellanos No. 85 (Madrid: La Lectura, 1958), p. 44.

11. See, for instance, Feijoo's essay, "Reflexiones sobre la historia" in *Teatro crítico universal* (Madrid, 1730).

12. See Feijoo's "Corruptibility of the Heavens" in *Teatro crítico universal*, VIII (Madrid, 1739).

13. For a fuller account of Porcel's "Moon-critique," see my *Origins of the Romantic Movement in Spain* (Liverpool: Institute of Hispanic Studies, 1937), pp. 47 ff.

14. This was on February 11, 1751. See *Actas* for that date.

15. For Papers submitted by Luzán in academic Disputations organized by the Real Academia de la Historia, see Bibliography, p. 191 below.

16. Juan Ignacio Luzán, *Vida*, ms, p. 72. Biblioteca Nacional, Madrid.

17. *Parnaso español* was published 1768–1771 in five volumes. Luzán figures in II, IV, and V. In addition to his long *Juicio de París* are some lighter verses including Anacreontics, some *canciones* and, in IV and V, some of his verse translations from Latin and Greek. Don Juan Ignacio's words appear to be taken directly from Sedano who, after praising Luzán's work, admits that in general his poetry depends "more on art than nature" and that, product of an artificial epoch, it has less robust verve than poetry of the previous centuries (*Parnaso español*, II, xii-xiii).

18. Juan Ignacio Luzán, *op. cit.*, p. 72.

19. "quejáronse las sombras asustadas." *BAE*, p. 112.

20. *BAE*, p. 120.

Chapter Three

1. *Memorias literarias de París* (Madrid: Ramírez, 1751). The pages of the Dedication and all other preliminaries are unnumbered. The Dedication is dated 29 December, 1750. See Introduction, p. 6.

2. *Memorias literarias de París*, p. 308.

3. See Chapter 4, p. 68 below.

4. See Chapter 2, p. 25 above.

5. *Memorias literarias de París*, Introduction, p. 2.

6. *Ibid.* p. 6.

7. J. Locke: *Some Thoughts Concerning Education* (London: Heinemann, 1969), p. 235.

8. Feijoo, *Teatro crítico universal*, ed. cit., Vol. I, No. 16.

9. Vives' Latin works have now been translated into Spanish. See *Obras completas*, 2 vols. (Madrid: Aguilar, 1947–1948). Luzán's reference will be to "Formación de la mujer cristiana . . ." in I, 989 ff.

10. See *Catalogue des Ouvrages mis à l'Index* (Paris: Imprimerie Ecclésiastique de Beaucé-Rusand, 1825). The first of Voltaire's works

to figure here is *Lettres Philosophiques* in 1752. Others follow rapidly.

11. *Memorias literarias de París*, p. 78.

12. *Ibid. Nanine* is based on Samuel Richardson's *Pamela*, first published in 1740.

13. See my *Spanish Drama of Pathos* (Liverpool: University Press, 1970), II, 472 *et passim*.

14. The reference is to Pierre-Louis Moreau de Maupertuis, a contemporary geometer. See *Memorias literarias de París*, p. 128.

15. See my *Spanish Drama of Pathos*, II, 426 ff.

16. See pp. 68 ff., below.

17. *Memorias literarias de París*, p. 84.

18. *Ibid.*, pp. 84–85.

19. *Ibid.*, pp. 84–86.

20. See my *Spanish Drama of Pathos*, I, 86–87.

21. *Memorias literarias de París*, pp. 119–22.

22. See *Vida . . . ms cit.*, pp. 70–71. The Spanish title of the projected work is: *Tratado del perfecto comediante*. It was to act as a complementary treatise to the *Poética*. D. Juan had seen his father's plan and chapter headings and considered that they embraced "everything necessary for acquiring perfection in the art" *(loc. cit.)*.

23. *Memorias literarias de París*, p. 122.

24. *Ibid.* See pp. 122 ff.

25. *Ibid.*, pp. 122–25.

26. *Ibid.*, p. 126.

27. *Ibid.*, pp. 126 ff.

28. See *Memorias literarias de París*, Chapter XIII, *passim*.

29. *Op. cit.*, pp. 131–32.

30. *Ibid.*, pp. 132–33.

31. *Ibid.*, p. 134.

32. *Loc. cit.*

33. The reference is to the sixteenth-century Spanish Jesuit and theologian, Francisco Suárez.

34. *Memorias literarias de París*, p. 175.

35. *Ibid.*, pp. 176–77.

36. *Ibid.*, p. 301.

37. *Ibid.*, pp. 301–2.

38. *Ibid.*, pp. 301–3.

39. *See Lettres de Thérèse . . . ou Mémoires d'une jeune Demoiselle de Province, pendant son séjour à Paris* (La Haye: J. Neaulme, 1740–1742), 2 vols.

40. It was published by Cramer, apparently in Geneva, in seven volumes. An editor's note in Vol. I of this edition explains that the author began to write it in 1740 and finished one version in 1749. The new version of 1756 gives additional material.

Chapter Four

1. On the cult of Metastasio in Spain, see e.g. E. Cotarelo y Mori, *Orígenes y establecimiento de la ópera en España hasta 1800* (Madrid: 1917); G. H. Stoudemire, "Metastasio in Spain," *Hispanic Review*, IX (1941), 184 ff; my *Origins of the Romantic Movement in Spain*, pp. 176 ff.

2. See *Vida*, pp. 101–2.

3. *Ibid.*, p. 101.

4. *Ibid.*, p. 102.

5. Directions to Act I. The manuscript has no pagination.

6. *Op. cit.*, Act III.

7. *Ibid.*, Act II. The change to a garden occurs within the Act.

8. See pp. 144–45 below.

9. See my *Spanish Drama of Pathos*, I, 268 ff.

10. *Virtud coronada*, Act I.

11. *Ibid.*

12. *Ibid.*

13. *Ibid.*

14. Luzán's title is *La clemencia de Tito* (Madrid: Mojados, 1747). The text is in Italian and Spanish. The music for the three acts is by three Italian musicians respectively.

15. Quazza's translation is entitled: *Clemencia de Tito* (Madrid, 1739).

16. Luzán, *op. cit.*, Act II, sc. viii. Compare Quazza, Act II, sc. vii.

17. Quazza, *op. cit.*, Act I, sc. viii. Compare Luzán, Act I, sc. ix.

18. Metastasio, *op. cit.*, Act III, sc. vi; Luzán, Act III, sc. vi., Quazza, Act III, sc. vi.

19. Nivelle de La Chaussée, *Le Préjugé à la mode* (Paris and Brussels: Lemmens, 1748). The Approbation is dated Paris, 1735, the date of the play's first performance. Luzán's translation is *La razón contra la moda* (Madrid, 1751).

20. The Dedication is addressed to the Marchioness of Sarria. The pages are not numbered.

21. See *Mémoires pour l'Histoire des Sciences et des Beaux Arts*, Trévoux, Jan., 1752, pp. 87–104.

22. See *Mémoires pour l'Histoire des Sciences . . . (ed. cit.)*, Jan., 1752, p. 92.

23. *Ibid.*, p. 88.

24. *Ibid.*, p. 94.

25. *Ibid.*, p. 92.

26. See my *Spanish Drama of Pathos*, I, 95.

27. Dedication to *La razón contra la moda (ed cit.)*.

Chapter Five

1. *La Poética, o reglas de la poesía en general, y de sus principales especies (Poetics, or Rules of Poetry in General and of the Principal Genres).* Zaragoza: Revilla, 1737. This edition has 503 pages with several unpaginated preliminaries.
La Poética. Second, augmented edition (Madrid: Sancha, 1789), 2 vols.

2. In this brief memorandum, the unnamed writer gives details of letters addressed by Don Juan to himself. They are readily identified with letters included in this collection and written to Llaguno. The writer also refers to his relationship with the elder Luzán, his own work as editor, and his own preface to the 1789 edition. The pages of the collection have been numbered in pencil.

3. See *Vida, BAE, ed. cit.,* LXI, 104.

4. *Ibid.* Also see pp. 175 ff., below.

5. *Ibid.,* and see *Poetics,* 1789, Vol. I, Book II, Chapter 3, 113. Luzán refers to Pope's *Essay on Man* as *El hombre (The Man).*

6. See the letter from Don Juan to Llaguno dated 29 February, 1780, p. 8.

7. There are reminders from Don Juan dated Segovia, 16 December, 1780, and Segovia, 3 February, 1781.

8. Llaguno's reply is dated at El Pardo, 21 February, 1781. It would appear to be his own copy of his letter to Don Juan and is not signed, or at least no signature appears on the surviving paper.

9. *Op. cit.* See p. 9 of the collection.

10. *Ibid.* See p. 1 of the collection.

11. *Ibid.*

12. See *Vida, BAE,* p. 105.

13. *Poetics,* 1789, Book I, Chapter 4, 33.

14. See *Vida, BAE,* p. 104.

Chapter Six

1. *Poética* (1737), p. 203.

2. *Aristotle's Theory of Poetry and Fine Art.* Translated and edited by S. H. Butcher, with a New Introduction by John Gassner (New York: Dover Publications, 1951), p. xxxix.

3. *De Arte Poetica.* Translated by H. R. Fairclough (London: Heinemann, and Harvard University Press, 1970), p. 479.

4. See P. Corneille, *Discours des trois unités d'action, de jour et de lieu* in *Trois Discours sur le Poème Dramatique* (from the 1660 text). Ed. Louis Forestier (Paris: Société d'Edition d'Enseignement Supérieur, 1963), III, 148.

5. Russell P. Sebold, "A Statistical Analysis of the Origins and Nature of Luzán's Ideas on Poetry," *Hispanic Review,* XXXV (July, 1967), 227–51.

6. J. Cano, *La Poética de Luzán* (Toronto: University of Toronto Press, 1928).

7. *Ibid.,* p. 20 (4).

8. Luzán, *Poética* (1737), Book III, Chap. II.

9. *Ibid.,* Book I, Chap. VII.

10. *Ibid.,* Book III, Chap. V.

11. *Ibid.,* p. 8.

Chapter Seven

1. This is from a lengthy "Approbation" which forms one of the preliminaries of the 1737 edition. There is no pagination.

2. See *Poetics* (1737), Preface. There is no pagination.

3. *Ibid.,* Chap. I, p. 5.

4. *Ibid.,* p. 1.

5. Aristotle, *ed. cit.,* p. 35.

6. Horace, *The Art of Poetry* (London: Everyman, 1934), p. 68.

7. See William Wordsworth's "Lines Composed a Few Miles Above Tintern Abbey."

8. *Poetics, ed. cit.,* p. 29.

9. *Ibid.,* p. 35.

10. *Ibid.,* p. 29.

11. L. A. Muratori, *Della perfetta poesia . . . , ed. cit.,* p. 73.

12. See Aristotle, *Poetics* (Cambridge: University Press, 1953), p. 11.

13. Aristotle, *Poetics, ed. cit.,* p. 11.

14. *Ibid.,* p. 116.

15. Horace, *The Art of Poetry, ed. cit.,* p. 71.

16. See *Republic.* Book X.

17. Luzán, *Poetics, ed. cit.,* p. 31.

18. *Ibid.,* p. 32.

19. *Ibid.,* p. 33.

20. *Poetics* (1789), I, 60.

21. Aristotle, *Poetics, ed. cit.,* pp. 116 ff.

22. *Ibid.,* and L. J. Potts, *Aristotle: Poetics* (Cambridge University Press, 1953), p. 9.

23. *Op. cit.,* p. 124.

24. Compare p. 96 above.

25. Luzán, *Poetics* (1737), p. 36.

26. *Ibid.,* p. 37.

27. *Ibid.,* pp. 39–40.

28. Aristotle, *Poetics,* p. 160.

29. J. G. Herder, *Sämmtliche Werke,* ed. Bernhard Suphan. 33 vols. (Berlin, 1877–1913). See V, 213.

30. Aristotle, *Poetics,* p. 101; Luzán, *op. cit.,* pp. 50–51.

31. Luzán, *op. cit.,* p. 52.

32. Compare Horace, *Art of Poetry,* ed. *cit.,* p. 71.

Chapter Eight

1. *Op. cit.,* p. 64.

2. *Ibid.,* p. 69.

3. *Ibid.,* p. 67.

4. *Ibid.,* p. 66.

5. William Wordsworth, "Lines Composed a Few Miles Above Tintern Abbey."

6. Luis de León, "Noche serena." See *Oxford Book of Spanish Verse* (Oxford, 1925), p. 114.

7. Luzán, *Poetics,* pp. 76 ff.

8. Luzán, *Poetics* (1737), pp. 77 ff.

9. *Ibid.,* p. 77.

10. *Ibid.,* p. 88.

11. *Ibid.* See Luzán's argument, pp. 93 ff.

12. *Ibid.,* p. 107.

13. *Ibid.,* pp. 102 ff.

14. *Ibid.,* pp. 109–10.

15. *Ibid.,* Chapter XI.

16. See pp. 35 ff., above.

17. *Poetics, ed. cit.,* pp. 117 ff.

18. See *Le Spectateur, ou Le Socrate Moderne.* Traduit de l'anglais, 7 vols. (Amsterdam and Leipzig, 1746–1750).

19. *Poetics,* pp. 126 ff.

20. *Ibid.,* p. 144.

21. *Ibid.,* pp. 127 ff.

22. *Ibid.,* pp. 144 ff.

23. *Ibid.,* p. 158.

24. *Ibid.*

25. *Ibid.* For these examples see pp. 163 ff.

26. See *Ibid.,* pp. 173 ff.

27. *Poetics, ed. cit.,* p. 181.

28. See B. J. Feijoo: *Teatro crítico universal,* Vol. III, Discourse 12. Biblioteca de Autores Españoles, CXLI (Madrid: Rivadeneira, 1961), 336. Feijoo's Vol. III was first published in 1729.

29. *Op. cit.,* p. 177.

Chapter Nine

1. *Aristotle, Poetics, ed. cit.*, pp. 247 ff. See p. 269.
2. *Ibid.*, p. 224.
3. *Ibid.*, pp. 224–25.
4. *Ibid.*, p. 245.
5. *Ibid.*, p. 248.
6. *Ibid.*, p. 23.
7. Luzán, *Poetics* (1737), pp. 277–78.
8. *Aristotle, Poetics*, pp. 27–29.
9. *Ibid.*, p. 31.
10. *Op. cit.*, Chapter IX, especially pp. 337, 346–47, 349.
11. Luzán, *Poetics* (1737), p. 281.
12. *Ibid.*, p. 284.
13. See p. 79 above.
14. See Bibliography, p. 191 below.
15. Luzán, *op. cit.*, p. 286.
16. *Ibid.*
17. *Ibid.*
18. See note 14 above.
19. Aristotle, *Poetics, ed. cit.*, p. 63.
20. Luzán, *Poetics, ed. cit.*, p. 288.
21. Aristotle, *Poetics, ed. cit.*, p. 89.
22. *Op. cit.*, pp. 276 ff.
23. The word "superstition" is Butcher's, *op. cit.*, p. 289.
24. See Aristotle, *Poetics*, ed. L. J. Potts (Cambridge: University Press, 1953), pp. 71 ff.
25. Aristotle, *Poetics*, ed. Gassner, p. 275.
26. *Op. cit.*, p. 23.
27. *Op. cit.*, p. XXXIX.
28. *Op. cit.*, pp. 294, 296.
29. *Op. cit.*, pp. 33 ff.
30. Luzán, *Poetics*, pp. 315–16.
31. *Ibid.*, p. 315.
32. *Ibid.*, p. 318.
33. See p. 62 above.
34. *Op. cit.*, p. 324.
35. *Ibid.* See both Chapters VII and VIII.
36. *Ibid.*, p. 354.
37. *Ibid.*, pp. 354–55.
38. *Ibid.*, p. 358.
39. *Aristotle, ed. cit.*, p. 233.
40. *Op. cit.*, p. 55.

Chapter Ten

1. Luzán, *Poetics* (1737), p. 8.
2. *Op. cit.*, p. 432.
3. *Ibid.*
4. See my *Benito Jerónimo Feijoo*, p. 102.
5. Luzán, *Poetics*, p. 465.
6. See B. J. Feijoo: *Teatro crítico universal*, VI (Madrid: Hierro, 1734), 350 *et passim*.
7. *Op. cit.*, p. 453. Compare my *Benito Jerónimo Feijoo*, pp. 78 ff.
8. See Nicolas Boileau, *L'Art poétique*, ed. cit., p. 80, lines 193 ff.

Chapter Eleven

1. See: *Mémoires pour l'Histoire des Sciences et des Beaux Arts*, ed. cit., II (May, 1748), 997–98. Review of Luzán's *Poetics*.
2. See "Aprobación." There is no pagination.
3. *Op. cit.* Compare Lope de Vega, *Arte nuevo de hacer comedias*, ed. cit., p. 22: *Yo hallo que, si allí se ha de dar gusto / con lo que se consigue es lo más justo.*
4. *Diario de los literatos de España* (Madrid: Antonio March and Imprenta Real, 1737–1742), 7 vols. See IV, 79–80.
5. *Ibid.*, p. 83.
6. See p. 125 above.
7. *Diario de los literatos de España*, IV, 97. The word is "desapasionado."
8. For details of the controversy between Neoclassicists and Nationalists, see my *Origins of the Romantic Movement in Spain*, pp. 7 ff.
9. *Op. cit.*, pp. 28 ff; pp. 54 ff.
10. See pp. 68 ff., above.
11. See *Vida*, p. 102.
12. The general title is: *Carta Latina . . . a los P.P. de Trévoux . . . Añádense dos cartas españolas sobre el mismo asunto*. See Bibliography under *Carta Latina . . .* p. 191 below. Don Juan also refers to another Apology written by Luzán in answer to the criticism of his *Poetics* in the *Journal of the Spanish Men of Letters*. He refers to it as a "discurso apologético," though he gives no exact title. He says that it was published in Pamplona in 1741, and that the notes which accompanied the text were by José Ignacio de Colmenares y Aramburu. Both used pseudonyms for the purpose: Don Ignacio called himself "Íñigo de Lanuza," and Don José used the name "Enrico Pío Gilasecas Modenés." So far we have been unable to trace this Apology. See *Vida*, p. 101.
13. *Op. cit.*, See the Latin section entitled *Epistola*.

14. *Op. cit.,* p. 33.

15. *Ibid.,* p. 44.

16. *Ibid.,* p. 48. The *Diario de los literatos de España* had criticized Luzán in these terms. See *Diario,* IV, 79–80, 99–100.

17. *Mémoires pour l'Histoire des Sciences et des Beaux Arts, ed. cit.,* II (May, 1748), 1024. The lines in Horace are: *Non satis est pulchra esse poemata; dulcia sunto / et quocumque volent animum auditoris agunto. De Arte Poetica* (London: Heinemann, and Harvard University Press, 1970), p. 458.

18. See Milton's Sonnet No. VII, "I did but prompt the age to quit their clogs." The line concerned is "Licence they mean when they cry liberty."

19. See pp. 68 ff., above.

20. For the work of both of these critics see pp. 89 ff., above and Bibliography.

Selected Bibliography

PRIMARY SOURCES

1. Luzán's Original Works in Chronological Order

La Poética (Zaragoza: Revilla, 1737). Second, augmented edition. 2 vols. (Madrid: Sancha, 1789).

La virtud coronada (1742). Manuscript. Academy of History, Madrid.

Carta Latina . . . a los Padres de Trévoux . . . (Zaragoza: Moreno, 1743).

La clemencia de Tito. Translated from Metastasio (Madrid: Mojados, 1747).

Memorias literarias de París (Madrid: Ramírez, 1751).

La razón contra la moda. From La Chaussée (Madrid, 1751).

El juicio de París, etc., in *Parnaso español.* . . . Ed. López de Sedano (Madrid: Ibarra, 1768–71). 15 vols. See vols. II, IV.

   Undated dissertations before the Academy of History are included in a collection of dissertations of the Academy in the National Library of Spain, Madrid. The collection has no general title page and bears no details of printing. See Luzán's "Disertación sobre el origen y patria primitiva de los godos," pp. 123–74 of the collection. Also "Disertación en que se demuestra que Ataulpho fue el primer rey godo de España . . . ," pp. 306–34 of the collection.

2. Modern Editions of Luzán's Work

Poesías. Biblioteca de Autores Españoles, LXI (Madrid: Rivadeneira, 1952).

La Poética. Ed. Luigi di Filippo. 2 vols. (Barcelona: Selecciones Bibliófilas, 1956). This is taken from the 1737 edition. The variants of the 1789 edition are given in an Appendix. The edition is prefaced with a useful study on Luzán's sources.

3. Eighteenth-century Treatises, Periodicals, etc., Discussed in the Present Volume

Actas de la Academia de Buen Gusto. Manuscript. National Library, Madrid. Collection of Pascual de Gayangos.

Cartas. Manuscript correspondence among Juan Ignacio Luzán, Eugenio de Llaguno, and R. de La Quadra concerning the publication of the second edition of the *Poética*. In the National Library, Madrid.

Diario de los literatos de España. 7 vols. (Madrid: Antonio Marín and Imprenta Real, 1737–1742).

FEIJOO, BENITO JERÓNIMO. *Teatro crítico universal*. 9 vols. (Madrid: Mojados and later Hierro, 1726–1740).

Journal des Savants. Founded by Denis de Sallo (Paris: 1665, etc.)

LUZÁN, JUAN IGNACIO. *Vida de Don Ignacio de Luzán*. Manuscript in the National Library, Madrid. Also a modern edition, slightly altered, in *Biblioteca de Autores Españoles, ed. cit.*, LXI.

LLAGUNO Y AMÍROLA, EUGENIO. *Apuntes para la historia de la poesía*. Manuscript in the National Library, Madrid.

Mémoires pour l'Histoire des Sciences et des Beaux Arts (Trévoux and Paris: Briasson and Chaubert, 1701, etc.)

METASTASIO, P.A.B.D. *Opere*. 17 vols. (Padua: Foglierini, 1811–1812).

MONTIANO y LUYANDO, AGUSTÍN. *Ataulpho* (Madrid, 1753), and *Virginia* (Madrid, 1750). Both accompanied by discourses.

NASARRE, B.A. *Comedias y entremeses de Miguel de Cervantes*. 2 vols. (Madrid, 1749).

NIVELLE DE LA CHAUSSÉE, P-C. *Le Préjugé à la Mode* (Paris and Brussels: Lemmens, 1748).

Parecer de los Srs Revisores sobre las tres Disertaciones de los Srs Huerta, Luzán y Ulloa sobre el primer rey godo que mandó en España, 16 Feb., 1760. Manuscript, Royal Academy of History, Madrid. The file (legajo 26) contains a packet of letters and Academic Judgments.

QUAZZA, P.P. *Clemencia de Tito* (Madrid, 1739).

Spectator, The. 4 vols. (1711–1714. Also London: Everyman, 1907–1934), Nos. 164–167.

THOMSON, JAMES. *The Complete Poetical Works* (London and New York: Oxford University Press, 1908).

4. Preceptists Discussed by Luzán and Given Prominence in the Present Volume

ARISTOTLE. *Poetics*. Ed. Butcher. Translation with Critical Notes (New York: Dover Publications, Inc., 1951).

———. *Poetics*. Ed. L. J. Potts (Cambridge: University Press, 1953).

BOILEAU, N. *Art Poétique* (Paris: Bordas, 1966).

CORNEILLE, P. *Trois Discours sur le poème Dramatique*. Ed. Forestier (Paris: Société d'Edition d'Enseignement Supérieur, 1963).

HORACE. *De Arte Poetica*. Ed. Fairclough (Harvard: Heinemann, 1970).

MURATORI, L.A. *Della perfetta poesia italiana*. In *Opere* in the Series *La Letteratura Italiana*. Ed. Mattioli, etc. (Milan-Naples: Ricciardi. Undated), Vol. XLIV.

Selected Bibliography

Vega Carpio, Lope Félix de. *Arte nuevo de hacer comedias.* In Chaytor's *Dramatic Theory in Spain* (Cambridge: University Press, 1925).

SECONDARY SOURCES

1. General Works on the Eighteenth Century in Spain

Cook, John A. *Neo-Classic Drama in Spain—Theory and Practice* (Dallas: Southern Methodist University Press, 1959). A work giving many helpful details in various fields of dramatic theory.

Delpy, G. *L'Espagne et l'esprit européen* (Paris: Hachette, 1936). A most useful book on Spain's literary relations with France and Europe generally.

Domínguez Ortiz, Antonio. *La sociedad española en el siglo XVIII* (Madrid: Consejo Superior de Investigaciones Científicas, 1955). An excellent work on the social and political background of Spain in the period.

Hazard, Paul. *European Thought in the Eighteenth Century* (London: Hollis and Carter, 1954). A capable discussion of the ideological background of the period in Europe generally.

Herr, Richard. *The Eighteenth-Century Revolution in Spain* (Princeton: University Press, 1958). A discussion of the ideological and technical changes in Spanish life in the century and an explanation of the reasons for such changes. A work essential to researchers on the period.

Menéndez y Pelayo, Marcelino. *Historia de las ideas estéticas en España* (Madrid: Colección de Escritores Castellanos, 1923), Vol. V. An introduction to the aesthetic problems of the period and to the work of Luzán. As always, this author has suggestions to aid modern researchers.

Pellissier, R. E. *The Neo-Classic Movement in Spain During the XVIII Century* (Stanford: The University Press, 1918). A good introduction to the meaning of Spanish Neoclassicism.

Sarrailh, Jean. *L'Espagne éclairée de la seconde moitié du XVIII siècle* (Paris: Klincksieck, 1954). A valuable study of the effects of Luzán's generation on its successor.

2. Interpretation and Criticism of Luzán

Cano, J. *La Poética de Luzán* (Toronto: University of Toronto Press, 1928). An essential book on Luzán dealing particularly with Italian influences on him.

Cerreta, F. V. "An Italian Source of Luzán's Theory of Tragedy," *Modern Language Notes.* LXXII (1957), 518–23. A further useful work on sources dealing especially with the influence on Luzán of A. Piccolomini.

Puppo, M. "Fonti italiane settecentesche della *Poética* de Luzán," *Lettere Italiane*, XIV (1962), 265–284. An additional treatise on Luzán's sources.

Sebold, R. P. "A Statistical Analysis of the Origins and Nature of Luzán's Ideas on Poetry," *Hispanic Review*, XXXV (July, 1967), 227–51. An indispensable, concise work on Luzán's sources, with very useful statistical tables. Dr. Sebold is preparing a new edition of the *Poética* for Textos Hispánicos Modernos, Editorial Labor, S.A. See also, by this author, *El rapto de la mente: poética española del siglo XVIII* (Madrid: Prensa Española, S.A.) on Luzán and related subjects, shortly to be published.

Index

(The works of Ignacio de Luzán are listed under his name)

Index

874/3

TWAYNE PUBLISHERS ANNOUNCE

The Spanish American Literature Section of Twayne's World Authors Series (TWAS), a program devoted to the critical assessment of major Spanish American writers of the past and present. Sylvia E. Bowman, Indiana University is General Editor of TWAS; John P. Dyson, Indiana University, is Editor of the Spanish American section; Irving Benowitz is Copy Editor.

MEXICO:

MARIANO AZUELA by Luis Leal (U. of Ill.)
SOR JUANA INES DE LA CRUZ by Gerald Flynn (U. of Wis.)
CARLOS FUENTES by Daniel de Guzman (Queens C.)
JAIME TORRES BODET by Sonja Karsen (Skidmore C.)
ALTAMIRANO by Chris N. Nacci (Capital U.)
XAVIER VILLAURRUTIA by Frank Dauster (Rutgers U.)

ARGENTINA:

ERNESTO SABATO by H. D. Oberhelman (Tex. Tech. U.)
SARMIENTO by Frances G. Crowley (Southeast Mo. St. C.)

CHILE:

EDUARDO BARRIOS by Ned J. Davison (U. of Utah)

PERU:

JOSE SANTOS CHOCANO by P. W. Rodriguez-Peralta (Temple U.)

GUATEMALA:

MIGUEL ANGEL ASTURIAS by Richard Callan (U. of New Hampshire)

For a Complete List of Books in This Open-end Series Write to:

TWAYNE PUBLISHERS, INC.
31 UNION SQUARE WEST   NEW YORK, N. Y. 10003

DATE DUE
